ArtScroll Series®

THE SCHOTTENSTEIN EDITION INTERLINEAR BIRCHON

Edited by
Rabbi Menachem Davis

Published by
Mesorah Publications, ltd

❦ TABLE OF CONTENTS ❦

בִּרְכַּת הַמָּזוֹן	3	Bircas HaMazon — Blessing After Meals
בְּרָכוֹת אַחֲרוֹנוֹת	24	Blessings After Other Foods
שֶׁבַע בְּרָכוֹת	26	Sheva Berachos
זִמּוּן לִסְעוּדַת הַבְּרִית	29	Zimun for the Circumcision Feast
קְרִיאַת שְׁמַע עַל הַמִּטָּה	33	The Bedtime Shema
תְּפִלַּת הַדֶּרֶךְ	46	The Wayfarer's Prayer

FIRST EDITION
Thirteen Impressions . . . November 2001 — December 2014

**THE ARTSCROLL® SERIES / SCHOTTENSTEIN EDITION
"THE ARTSCROLL INTERLINEAR BIRCHON"**
© *Copyright 2001, by* MESORAH PUBLICATIONS, Ltd.
4401 Second Avenue / Brooklyn, N.Y. 11232 / (718) 921-9000 / www.artscroll.com

ALL RIGHTS RESERVED. *The Hebrew text, punctuation and format, the new translation, commentary, instructions, prefatory and associated textual contents and introductions — including the typographic layout, cover artwork, and ornamental graphics — have been designed, edited and revised as to content, form and style.*

**No part of this book may be reproduced
IN ANY FORM — PHOTOCOPY, ELECTRONIC, DIGITAL MEDIA, OR OTHERWISE —
EVEN FOR PERSONAL, OR SYNAGOGUE USE — without WRITTEN permission from the copyright holder,**
*except by a reviewer who wishes to quote brief passages
in connection with a review written for inclusion in magazines or newspapers.*

PATENT NOTICE
NOTICE IS HEREBY GIVEN THAT MANY ADDITIONAL WORKS IN THIS INTERLINEAR FORMAT
ARE IN PROGRESS, INVOLVING RESEARCH AND GREAT EXPENSE.
THE PAGE LAYOUT, AND THE VISUAL SYMBOLS AND GRAPHICS IN ALL THEIR FORMS,
HAVE BEEN REGISTERED, AND UNITED STATES PATENT 6778950 HAS BEEN GRANTED
IN ADDITION TO AN INTERNATIONAL COPYRIGHT.
THE RIGHTS OF THE COPYRIGHT AND PATENT OWNER WILL BE STRICTLY ENFORCED.

Copper — ISBN 10: 1-57819-696-5 / ISBN 13: 978-1-57819-696-8
White Blank — ISBN 10: 1-57819-684-1 / ISBN 13: 978-1-57819-684-5
White Stamped — ISBN 10: 1-57819-683-3 / ISBN 13: 978-1-57819-683-8

*Typography by CompuScribe at ArtScroll Studios, Ltd., Brooklyn, NY
Bound by* **Sefercraft, Inc.,** *Brooklyn, NY*

◈ BLESSING AFTER MEALS / ברכת המזון ◈

IT IS CUSTOMARY TO RECITE PSALM 137 BEFORE *BIRCAS HAMAZON* ON THE WEEKDAYS.

עַל נַהֲרוֹת בָּבֶל, שָׁם יָשַׁבְנוּ, גַּם בָּכִינוּ, בְּזָכְרֵנוּ
⟨ when we remembered ⟨⟨ we wept ⟨ and also ⟨ we sat ⟨ there ⟨ of Babylon, ⟨ the rivers ⟨ By

אֶת צִיּוֹן. עַל עֲרָבִים בְּתוֹכָהּ, תָּלִינוּ כִּנֹּרוֹתֵינוּ. כִּי שָׁם
⟨ there For ⟨⟨ our lyres. ⟨ we hung ⟨ within it ⟨ the willows ⟨ On ⟨⟨ Zion.

שְׁאֵלוּנוּ שׁוֹבֵינוּ דִּבְרֵי שִׁיר וְתוֹלָלֵינוּ שִׂמְחָה, שִׁירוּ לָנוּ
⟨ for us Sing ⟨⟨ joyous music: ⟨ with our lyres [playing] ⟨ of words ⟨ song, ⟨ did our captors ⟨ request from us

מִשִּׁיר צִיּוֹן. אֵיךְ נָשִׁיר אֶת שִׁיר יהוה, עַל אַדְמַת נֵכָר.
⟨⟨ of an alien [god]? ⟨ the soil ⟨ upon ⟨ of ⟨ the song ⟨ can we ⟨ How ⟨⟨ of ⟨ from Zion! HASHEM the songs

אִם אֶשְׁכָּחֵךְ יְרוּשָׁלָיִם, תִּשְׁכַּח יְמִינִי. תִּדְבַּק לְשׁוֹנִי
⟨ let my tongue ⟨ Adhere ⟨⟨ let my right hand [its skill]. ⟨ [then] forget ⟨ O Jerusalem, ⟨ I forget you, ⟨ If

לְחִכִּי, אִם לֹא אֶזְכְּרֵכִי; אִם לֹא אַעֲלֶה אֶת יְרוּשָׁלַיִם
⟨ Jerusalem ⟨ I fail to elevate ⟨ if ⟨⟨ I fail to remember you, ⟨ if ⟨ to my palate,

עַל רֹאשׁ שִׂמְחָתִי. זְכֹר יהוה לִבְנֵי אֱדוֹם אֵת יוֹם
⟨ the day ⟨ [to repay] the offspring of Edom, ⟨ HASHEM, ⟨ Remember, ⟨⟨ of my joys. ⟨ the foremost ⟨ above

יְרוּשָׁלָיִם; הָאֹמְרִים עָרוּ עָרוּ, עַד הַיְסוֹד בָּהּ. בַּת בָּבֶל
⟨ of ⟨ O ⟨⟨ of it. ⟨ the very foundation ⟨ to ⟨ Destroy! ⟨ Destroy! ⟨⟨ [to repay] ⟨ of Jerusalem; Babylon daughter ⟨ those who say,

הַשְּׁדוּדָה, אַשְׁרֵי שֶׁיְּשַׁלֶּם לָךְ אֶת גְּמוּלֵךְ שֶׁגָּמַלְתְּ לָנוּ.
⟨⟨ us. ⟨ for how you treated ⟨ your recompense ⟨ you ⟨ is the one who repays ⟨ praise-worthy ⟨ who has been violated,

אַשְׁרֵי שֶׁיֹּאחֵז וְנִפֵּץ אֶת עֹלָלַיִךְ אֶל הַסָּלַע.
⟨⟨ the rock. ⟨ against ⟨ your infants ⟨ and dash ⟨ the one who will clutch ⟨ Praiseworthy will be

---

◈ ברכת המזון / **BLESSING AFTER MEALS** ◈

The commandment to thank God after a meal is of Scriptural origin: וְאָכַלְתָּ וְשָׂבָעְתָּ וּבֵרַכְתָּ אֶת ה' אֱלֹהֶיךָ עַל הָאָרֶץ הַטֹּבָה אֲשֶׁר נָתַן לָךְ, *And you shall eat and you shall be satisfied and you shall bless* HASHEM, *your God, for the good Land that He gave you* (Deuteronomy 8:10). As the verse indicates, the Scriptural requirement applies only when one has eaten his fill — *you shall eat and you shall be satisfied*. From earliest times, however, the Jewish people have undertaken to express their gratitude to God even after a modest meal, provided one had eaten at least as much bread as the volume of an olive [כְּזַיִת].

IT IS CUSTOMARY TO RECITE PSALM 126 BEFORE *BIRCAS HAMAZON* ON THE SABBATH AND FESTIVALS, ON DAYS WHEN *TACHANUN* IS NOT SAID, AND AT FESTIVE MEALS SUCH AS A WEDDING, A *BRIS*, OR A *PIDYON HABEN*.

שִׁיר הַמַּעֲלוֹת; בְּשׁוּב יהוה אֶת שִׁיבַת צִיּוֹן, הָיִינוּ
⟨ we will be ⟨⟨ of ⟨ captivity ⟨ the ⟨ When Hashem will return ⟨⟨ of ascents. ⟨ A song

כְּחֹלְמִים. אָז יִמָּלֵא שְׂחוֹק פִּינוּ, וּלְשׁוֹנֵנוּ רִנָּה; אָז
⟨ Then ⟨⟨ with and our glad song. ⟨ our tongue ⟨⟨ with mouth, ⟨ filled ⟨ with will be laughter ⟨ Then ⟨⟨ like dreamers.

יֹאמְרוּ בַגּוֹיִם: הִגְדִּיל יהוה לַעֲשׂוֹת עִם אֵלֶּה. הִגְדִּיל
⟨ Greatly ⟨⟨ these. ⟨ with ⟨ done ⟨ has Hashem ⟨ Greatly ⟨⟨ among the nations, ⟨ will they declare

יהוה לַעֲשׂוֹת עִמָּנוּ, הָיִינוּ שְׂמֵחִים. שׁוּבָה יהוה
⟨ O Hashem, ⟨ Return, ⟨⟨ gladdened. ⟨ we were ⟨⟨ with us, ⟨ done ⟨ has Hashem

אֶת שְׁבִיתֵנוּ, כַּאֲפִיקִים בַּנֶּגֶב. הַזֹּרְעִים בְּדִמְעָה, בְּרִנָּה
⟨ with glad song ⟨⟨ tearfully, ⟨ Those who sow ⟨⟨ in the desert. ⟨ like springs ⟨⟨ our captivity,

יִקְצֹרוּ. הָלוֹךְ יֵלֵךְ וּבָכֹה נֹשֵׂא מֶשֶׁךְ הַזָּרַע; בֹּא יָבֹא
⟨ he will return ⟨ but ⟨⟨ return ⟨ of seeds, ⟨ the measure ⟨⟨ does he carries ⟨ weeping, ⟨ he walks ⟨ Walk on, ⟨⟨ will reap.

בְרִנָּה, נֹשֵׂא אֲלֻמֹּתָיו.
⟨⟨ of his sheaves. ⟨ a bearer ⟨⟨ in exultation,

There are several opinions regarding the modern equivalent of this Talmudic measurement; they range from one, to one and four-fifths fluid ounces.

The first to compose a text for Blessing After Meals was Moses, whose text is still recited as the first blessing. Although Moses' blessing was composed in gratitude for the manna in the Wilderness, it makes no mention of the manna. It is equally noteworthy that the commandment of Blessing After Meals (cited above) was given in the context of a general exhortation to Israel that they remember the heavenly food with which God nourished them in the Wilderness. The message seems obvious: When we thank God for giving us food, we are recognizing that there is no intrinsic difference between the manna and the livelihood one wrests from the earth through sweat and hard toil; both are gifts from heaven.

שִׁיר הַמַּעֲלוֹת / Psalm 126

This is one of the fifteen psalms (*Psalms* 120-134) known as the *Songs of Ascents*. The "ascents" correspond to the fifteen steps leading to the inner courtyard of the Temple. As the procession ascended into the holy area with water for the special service of *Succos*, the Levites would stand on the steps singing each of the fifteen psalms in turn.

The commentators note that all fifteen psalms refer to Jewish prayers that we may "ascend" from exile and return to *Eretz Yisrael* and a rebuilt Temple. *R' S. R. Hirsch* comments that they are like a spiritual ladder of fifteen steps, designed to help a Jew climb out of the misery of oppressive circumstances.

5 / BLESSING AFTER MEALS — ZIMUN

תְּהִלַּת יהוה יְדַבֶּר פִּי, וִיבָרֵךְ כָּל בָּשָׂר שֵׁם קָדְשׁוֹ
‹ of His Holiness ‹ the Name ‹ flesh ‹ may ‹ and bless ‹ may my mouth declare, ‹ of Hashem ‹ The praise

לְעוֹלָם וָעֶד.[1] וַאֲנַחְנוּ נְבָרֵךְ יָהּ, מֵעַתָּה וְעַד עוֹלָם,
‹ eternity, ‹ until ‹ from this time ‹ God ‹ will bless ‹ But we ‹ and ever. ‹ forever

הַלְלוּיָהּ.[2] הוֹדוּ לַיהוה כִּי טוֹב, כִּי לְעוֹלָם חַסְדּוֹ.[3] מִי
‹ Who ‹ is His enduring kindness! ‹ forever ‹ for ‹ He is ‹ for ‹ to Hashem ‹ Give thanks ‹ Hallelujah!

יְמַלֵּל גְּבוּרוֹת יהוה, יַשְׁמִיעַ כָּל תְּהִלָּתוֹ.[4]
‹ of His praise? ‹ all ‹ [who] can make heard ‹ of Hashem, ‹ the mighty acts ‹ can express

הִנְנִי מוּכָן וּמְזֻמָּן לְקַיֵּם מִצְוַת עֲשֵׂה שֶׁל בִּרְכַּת
‹ Blessing ‹ of ‹ the positive commandment ‹ to perform ‹ and ready ‹ am ‹ I now

הַמָּזוֹן, שֶׁנֶּאֱמַר: וְאָכַלְתָּ וְשָׂבָעְתָּ, וּבֵרַכְתָּ אֶת יהוה
‹ Hashem, ‹ and you shall bless ‹ and you shall be satisfied ‹ And you shall eat ‹ for it is said: ‹ Meals, ‹ after

אֱלֹהֶיךָ, עַל הָאָרֶץ הַטֹּבָה אֲשֶׁר נָתַן לָךְ.[5]
‹ you. ‹ He gave ‹ which ‹ that is good ‹ the land ‹ for ‹ your God,

ZIMUN/INVITATION / זימון

IF THREE OR MORE MALES, AGED THIRTEEN OR OLDER, PARTICIPATE IN A MEAL, A LEADER IS APPOINTED TO FORMALLY INVITE THE OTHERS TO JOIN HIM IN THE RECITATION OF *BIRCAS HAMAZON*. WHEN *ZIMUN* IS RECITED, IT IS PREFERABLE FOR THE LEADER TO HOLD A CUP OF WINE (O.C. 182). (ON CERTAIN OCCASIONS A SPECIAL *ZIMUN* IS RECITED: FOR *SHEVA BERACHOS* SEE PAGE 26, FOR THE CIRCUMCISION FEAST SEE PAGE 29.) THE REGULAR *ZIMUN* FOLLOWS.

Leader – רַבּוֹתַי מִיר וֶועלֶן בֶּענְטשֶׁען [רַבּוֹתַי נְבָרֵךְ].
‹ [let us bless. ‹ Gentlemen,] ‹ bless. ‹ let us ‹ Gentlemen,

Others – יְהִי שֵׁם יהוה מְבֹרָךְ מֵעַתָּה וְעַד עוֹלָם.[6]
‹ eternity. ‹ until ‹ from this time ‹ be blessed ‹ of Hashem ‹ the Name ‹ Let

Leader – יְהִי שֵׁם יהוה מְבֹרָךְ* מֵעַתָּה וְעַד עוֹלָם.[6]
‹ eternity. ‹ until ‹ from this time ‹ be blessed* ‹ of Hashem ‹ the Name ‹ Let

(1) *Psalms* 145:21. (2) 115:18. (3) 118:1. (4) 106:2. (5) *Deuteronomy* 8:10. (6) *Psalms* 113:2.

∽§ זימון / Zimun (Invitation)

The word *zimun* connotes both *invitation* and *presentation*. When three or more people eat together, one *invites* the others to respond to his praise of God; and all of them jointly are required to *present* themselves as a group to come together in praise of God (based on *Berachos* 49b).

יְהִי שֵׁם ה׳ מְבֹרָךְ — *Let the Name of Hashem be blessed.* The leader, too, repeats the blessings because it would be improper and even sacrilegious for him to ask others to bless God while he, being part of the group, refrains from joining them (*Rashba*).

IF TEN MEN JOIN IN THE ZIMUN, AMONG WHOM AT LEAST SEVEN ATE BREAD, ADD GOD'S NAME (IN PARENTHESES).

בִּרְשׁוּת* מָרָנָן וְרַבָּנָן וְרַבּוֹתַי, נְבָרֵךְ* (אֱלֹהֵינוּ)* שֶׁאָכַלְנוּ מִשֶּׁלּוֹ.*

With the permission* ⟩ of the distin- ⟩ and ⟩ and ⟩ let us bless* ⟩ (our God,) ⟩⟩ for we have eaten. ⟩ of what is His.*
guished people rabbis gentlemen, [Him,]

בָּרוּךְ (אֱלֹהֵינוּ) שֶׁאָכַלְנוּ מִשֶּׁלּוֹ וּבְטוּבוֹ חָיִינוּ. — Others

Blessed ⟩ (our God,) ⟩ for we ⟩ of what ⟩ and through ⟩ we
is [He,] have eaten is His His goodness live.

THOSE WHO HAVE NOT EATEN RESPOND:

בָּרוּךְ (אֱלֹהֵינוּ) וּמְבֹרָךְ שְׁמוֹ תָּמִיד לְעוֹלָם וָעֶד.

Blessed ⟩ (our God,) ⟩ and ⟩ is His ⟩ continuously ⟩ for ever ⟩⟩ and
is [He,] blessed Name ever.

בָּרוּךְ (אֱלֹהֵינוּ) שֶׁאָכַלְנוּ מִשֶּׁלּוֹ וּבְטוּבוֹ חָיִינוּ. — Leader

Blessed ⟩ (our God,) ⟩ for we ⟩ of what ⟩ and through ⟩ we
is [He,] have eaten is His His goodness live.

(בָּרוּךְ הוּא וּבָרוּךְ שְׁמוֹ.)

(Blessed ⟩ is He ⟩ and Blessed ⟩⟩ is His Name.)

THE ZIMUN LEADER RECITES THE BLESSING AFTER MEALS (AT LEAST THE FIRST BLESSING AND THE CONCLUSION OF THE OTHERS) ALOUD. ASIDE FROM RESPONDING AMEN AT THE CONCLUSION OF EACH BLESSING, IT IS FORBIDDEN TO INTERRUPT THE BLESSING AFTER MEALS FOR ANY RESPONSE OTHER THAN THOSE PERMITTED DURING THE SHEMA.

FIRST BLESSING: FOR THE NOURISHMENT / הַבְּרָכָה הָרִאשׁוֹנָה — בִּרְכַּת הַזָּן

בָּרוּךְ אַתָּה יהוה אֱלֹהֵינוּ מֶלֶךְ הָעוֹלָם,

Blessed ⟩ are You, ⟩ HASHEM, ⟩ our God, ⟩ King ⟩⟩ of the universe,

בִּרְשׁוּת — *With the permission.* Since one of the group assumes the privilege of leading them all in the recitation, he requests their permission.

נְבָרֵךְ — *Let us bless.* A commandment done by an individual cannot be compared to one performed by a group. When three men recite *Bircas HaMazon* together, they say נְבָרֵךְ, *let us bless*; ten men say, נְבָרֵךְ אֱלֹהֵינוּ, *let us bless our God …* (*Berachos* 49b. See also *Rashi, Lev.* 26:8). When many people unite to do God's will, each individual in the group reaches a far higher level than he would have had he acted alone, no matter how meritoriously he had acted (*Chofetz Chaim*).

שֶׁאָכַלְנוּ מִשֶּׁלּוֹ — *For we have eaten of what is His.* This text is drawn from Abraham. He would invite wayfarers to his home and serve them lavishly. When they were sated and refreshed and ready to continue on their way, they would thank him. He would insist that their thanks go not to him, but to God, the One from Whose bounty they had eaten (*Sotah* 10b; *Iyun Tefillah*).

בִּרְכַּת הַזָּן /
First Blessing: For the Nourishment

Bircas HaMazon comprises four blessings, of which the first three are Scripturally ordained and the fourth was instituted by the Sages. The first blessing was, as noted above,

7 / BLESSING AFTER MEALS

הַזָּן אֶת הָעוֹלָם כֻּלּוֹ, בְּטוּבוֹ, בְּחֵן בְּחֶסֶד וּבְרַחֲמִים, הוּא נֹתֵן לֶחֶם לְכָל בָּשָׂר, כִּי לְעוֹלָם חַסְדּוֹ.[1] וּבְטוּבוֹ הַגָּדוֹל, תָּמִיד לֹא חָסַר לָנוּ, וְאַל יֶחְסַר לָנוּ* מָזוֹן לְעוֹלָם וָעֶד. בַּעֲבוּר שְׁמוֹ הַגָּדוֹל,* כִּי הוּא אֵל זָן וּמְפַרְנֵס* לַכֹּל, וּמֵטִיב* לַכֹּל, וּמֵכִין מָזוֹן לְכָל בְּרִיּוֹתָיו אֲשֶׁר בָּרָא. (כָּאָמוּר: פּוֹתֵחַ אֶת יָדֶךָ, וּמַשְׂבִּיעַ לְכָל חַי רָצוֹן.[2]) ❖ בָּרוּךְ אַתָּה יהוה, הַזָּן אֶת הַכֹּל. (אָמֵן – Others).

《 Who nourishes 》 the world, 《 all of it, 》 in His goodness, 《 with grace, 》 – with kindness, and with compassion. 《 He 》 gives 《 food 》 to all 《 flesh, 》 for 《 forever 》 is His kindness. 《 And through His goodness that is great, 》 never 《 have we lacked, 》 and never 《 may we lack,* 》 nourishment, 《 for ever 》 and ever. 《 For the sake 》 of His Name 《 that is great,* 》 because 《 He 》 is 《 God 》 nourishes* 《 and sustains* 》 all, 《 and benefits* 》 all, 《 and He prepares 》 nourishment 《 for all 》 of His creatures 《 which 》 He has created. 《 (As it is said, 》 You open 《 Your hand, 》 and satisfy 《 every 》 living thing 《 [with its] desire.》 ❖ Blessed 《 are You, 》 HASHEM, 《 Who nourishes 》 all. 《 (Amen.) 》

(1) Psalms 136:25. (2) 145:16.

composed by Moses in gratitude for the manna with which God sustained Israel daily in the desert (Berachos 48b). For that reason it precedes בִּרְכַּת הָאָרֶץ, the Blessing for the Land, even though it might seem more logical to thank God first for the land that produces food (Bayis Chadash).

תָּמִיד לֹא חָסַר לָנוּ וְאַל יֶחְסַר לָנוּ — Never have we lacked, and never may we lack. The subject of the sentence is מָזוֹן, nourishment, and the verse expresses the prayer that just as food was never lacking in the desert, may it never be lacking in the future (Etz Yosef).

בַּעֲבוּר שְׁמוֹ הַגָּדוֹל — For the sake of His Name that is great. We declare that the motive for our request for eternally abundant food is but for the sake of His Name that is great so that we may be better able to serve Him; and we bless Him because...

זָן ... וּמְפַרְנֵס ... וּמֵטִיב — Who nourishes ... sustains ... benefits. זָן, nourishes, refers to food; מְפַרְנֵס, sustains, refers to clothing; מֵטִיב, benefits, refers to shelter. In conjunction the three phrases enumerate the basic needs of life, all of which are provided by God (Etz Yosef).

SECOND BLESSING: FOR THE LAND / הַבְּרָכָה הַשְּׁנִיָּה – בִּרְכַּת הָאָרֶץ

נוֹדֶה לְךָ יהוה אֱלֹהֵינוּ, עַל שֶׁהִנְחַלְתָּ
We thank › You, › Hashem, › our God, ›› because › You have given as a heritage

לַאֲבוֹתֵינוּ* אֶרֶץ חֶמְדָּה טוֹבָה וּרְחָבָה,* וְעַל
to our forefathers* › a Land, › desirable, › good, › and spacious;* ›› because ›

שֶׁהוֹצֵאתָנוּ יהוה אֱלֹהֵינוּ מֵאֶרֶץ מִצְרַיִם,
You brought us out, › Hashem, › our God, ›› from the land › of Egypt ››

וּפְדִיתָנוּ מִבֵּית עֲבָדִים, וְעַל בְּרִיתְךָ שֶׁחָתַמְתָּ
and You redeemed us › from the house › of bondage; ›› for › Your covenant › which You sealed

בִּבְשָׂרֵנוּ,* וְעַל תּוֹרָתְךָ שֶׁלִּמַּדְתָּנוּ, וְעַל חֻקֶּיךָ
in our flesh;* ›› for › Your Torah › which You taught us, ›› and for › Your statutes

שֶׁהוֹדַעְתָּנוּ, וְעַל חַיִּים חֵן וָחֶסֶד שֶׁחוֹנַנְתָּנוּ,
which You made known to us; ›› for › life, › grace, › and lovingkindness › which You granted us,

וְעַל אֲכִילַת מָזוֹן שָׁאַתָּה זָן וּמְפַרְנֵס אוֹתָנוּ
and for › [our] eating › of the food › with which › You › nourish › and sustain › us

תָּמִיד, בְּכָל יוֹם וּבְכָל עֵת וּבְכָל שָׁעָה.
constantly, ›› in every › day, › in every › time, › and in every › hour.

בִּרְכַּת הָאָרֶץ / Second Blessing: For the Land

The second blessing was also ordained by the Torah [*Deut.* 8:10, see *Overview* to ArtScroll *Bircas HaMazon*] and formulated by Joshua (*Berachos* 48a). He saw how deeply Moses desired to enter *Eretz Yisrael*, and how eager the Patriarchs were to be buried there. When Joshua was privileged to enter *Eretz Yisrael*, he composed this blessing in honor of the Land (*Shibolei HaLeket*).

The blessing begins and ends with thanks. The expression of gratitude refers to each of the enumerated items: the Land, the Exodus, the covenant, the Torah, the statutes, life, grace, kindness, and food.

שֶׁהִנְחַלְתָּ לַאֲבוֹתֵינוּ — *You have given as a heritage to our forefathers. Eretz Yisrael* is referred to as נַחֲלָה, *a heritage*, implying that it remains eternally our inheritance. Thus, the long exile means only that God has denied us access in punishment for our sins, not that it has ceased to be ours.

חֶמְדָּה טוֹבָה וּרְחָבָה — *Desirable, good, and spacious.* Whoever does not say that the Land is *desirable, good,* and *spacious* has not properly fulfilled his obligation [of *Bircas HaMazon*] (*Berachos* 48b), because once the Torah required that the Land be mentioned, the Sages decreed that its praises should likewise be enumerated (*Talmidei R' Yonah*).

וְעַל בְּרִיתְךָ שֶׁחָתַמְתָּ בִּבְשָׂרֵנוּ — *For Your covenant*

9 / BLESSING AFTER MEALS

ON CHANUKAH AND PURIM ADD THE FOLLOWING.

(וְ)עַל הַנִּסִּים, וְעַל הַפֻּרְקָן, וְעַל הַגְּבוּרוֹת, וְעַל
‹ and for ‹ the mighty deeds, ‹ and for ‹ the salvation, ‹ and for ‹ the miracles, ‹ (And) for

הַתְּשׁוּעוֹת, (וְעַל הַנִּפְלָאוֹת, וְעַל הַנֶּחָמוֹת,) וְעַל הַמִּלְחָמוֹת,
‹ the battles ‹ and for ‹ the consolations, ‹ and for ‹ the wonders, ‹ and for ‹ the victories,

שֶׁעָשִׂיתָ לַאֲבוֹתֵינוּ בַּיָּמִים הָהֵם בַּזְּמַן הַזֶּה.
« at this time: ‹ in those days, « for our forefathers ‹ that You performed

ON CHANUKAH:

בִּימֵי מַתִּתְיָהוּ בֶּן יוֹחָנָן כֹּהֵן גָּדוֹל חַשְׁמוֹנָאִי וּבָנָיו,
« and his « the ‹ the High Priest, ‹ of ‹ the « of ‹ In the
sons, Hasmonean, Yochanan, son Mattisyahu, days

כְּשֶׁעָמְדָה מַלְכוּת יָוָן הָרְשָׁעָה עַל עַמְּךָ יִשְׂרָאֵל, לְהַשְׁכִּיחָם
‹ to make ‹ Israel, ‹ Your ‹ against ‹‹–which was ‹‹ of ‹ did the ‹ when rise up
them forget people wicked– Greece kingdom

תּוֹרָתֶךָ, וּלְהַעֲבִירָם מֵחֻקֵּי רְצוֹנֶךָ. וְאַתָּה בְּרַחֲמֶיךָ
‹ in Your ‹ But You « of Your Will. ‹ from the ‹ and to compel « Your
compassion statutes them to stray Torah

הָרַבִּים, עָמַדְתָּ לָהֶם בְּעֵת צָרָתָם, רַבְתָּ אֶת רִיבָם, דַּנְתָּ
‹ judged ‹ their cause, ‹ You ‹ of their ‹ in the ‹ for ‹ stood up « which is
championed distress. time them abundant

אֶת דִּינָם, נָקַמְתָּ אֶת נִקְמָתָם.¹ מָסַרְתָּ גִבּוֹרִים בְּיַד חַלָּשִׁים,
« of the ‹ into the ‹ the strong ‹ You « their wrong. ‹ and You « their claim,
weak, hands delivered avenged

וְרַבִּים בְּיַד מְעַטִּים, וּטְמֵאִים בְּיַד טְהוֹרִים, וּרְשָׁעִים בְּיַד
‹ into the ‹ the wicked « of the pure, ‹ into the ‹ the impure « of the few, ‹ into the ‹ the
hands hands hands many

צַדִּיקִים, וְזֵדִים בְּיַד עוֹסְקֵי תוֹרָתֶךָ. וּלְךָ עָשִׂיתָ שֵׁם גָּדוֹל
‹ that ‹ a ‹ You ‹ For ‹ of Your ‹ of the ‹ into the ‹ and the ‹ of the
is great Name made Yourself Torah. diligent hands willful righteous
students sinners

וְקָדוֹשׁ בְּעוֹלָמֶךָ, וּלְעַמְּךָ יִשְׂרָאֵל עָשִׂיתָ תְּשׁוּעָה גְדוֹלָה²
‹ of great ‹ a victory ‹ You ‹ Israel ‹ and for ‹ in Your ‹ and holy
magnitude performed Your people world,

---

(1) Cf. *Jeremiah* 51:36. (2) Cf. *I Samuel* 19:5.

which You sealed in our flesh. The reference is to circumcision, of which the Sages required mention in the blessing of the Land (*Berachos* 48b) because the Land was promised to Abraham in the merit of circumcision (*Genesis* 17:7-8).

Women are not subject to the commandments of circumcision and Torah study. Nevertheless, women do say, *For Your covenant which You*

וּפֻרְקָן כְּהַיּוֹם הַזֶּה. וְאַחַר כֵּן בָּאוּ בָנֶיךָ לִדְבִיר בֵּיתֶךָ,
and a « as this very day. » Thereafter, « came » Your « to the Holy « of Your
salvation   children of Holies House,

וּפִנּוּ אֶת הֵיכָלֶךָ, וְטִהֲרוּ אֶת מִקְדָּשֶׁךָ, וְהִדְלִיקוּ נֵרוֹת
« lights « and kindled « Your holy site, » purified « Your Temple, « cleansed

בְּחַצְרוֹת קָדְשֶׁךָ, וְקָבְעוּ שְׁמוֹנַת יְמֵי חֲנֻכָּה אֵלּוּ,
«—these—« of « the eight « and they « of Your « in the
   Chanukah   days   established Sanctuary;   Courtyards

לְהוֹדוֹת וּלְהַלֵּל לְשִׁמְךָ הַגָּדוֹל.
« that is great. « to Your « and praise « to express
                     Name   thanks

ON PURIM:

בִּימֵי מָרְדְּכַי וְאֶסְתֵּר בְּשׁוּשַׁן הַבִּירָה, כְּשֶׁעָמַד עֲלֵיהֶם
« against « when « the capital, « in   « and « of   « In the
   them   rise up   Shushan, Esther, Mordechai days

הָמָן הָרָשָׁע, בִּקֵּשׁ לְהַשְׁמִיד לַהֲרֹג וּלְאַבֵּד אֶת כָּל הַיְּהוּדִים,
« the Jews, « all « and to « to slay, « to destroy, « he « the « did
                      exterminate   sought wicked Haman,

מִנַּעַר וְעַד זָקֵן, טַף וְנָשִׁים בְּיוֹם אֶחָד, בִּשְׁלוֹשָׁה עָשָׂר
« on the thirteenth [day] « on the same day, « and « infants « old, « to « from
                                                    women,   young

לְחֹדֶשׁ שְׁנֵים עָשָׂר, הוּא חֹדֶשׁ אֲדָר, וּשְׁלָלָם לָבוֹז.[1]
« to be « and their « of Adar, « the « which « twelve « of month
plundered possessions   month   is

וְאַתָּה בְּרַחֲמֶיךָ הָרַבִּים הֵפַרְתָּ אֶת עֲצָתוֹ, וְקִלְקַלְתָּ
« and « his counsel, « nullified « which is « in Your mercy « But You,
frustrated   abundant,

אֶת מַחֲשַׁבְתּוֹ, וַהֲשֵׁבוֹתָ לּוֹ גְּמוּלוֹ בְּרֹאשׁוֹ, וְתָלוּ אוֹתוֹ
« him « and they « upon his « his « to « and « his intention,
        hanged   own head, recompense him returned

וְאֶת בָּנָיו עַל הָעֵץ.
« the gallows. « on « and his sons

---

(1) *Esther* 3:13.

sealed in our flesh; for Your Torah which You taught us. Magen Avraham explains that since women do not require circumcision, they are considered as equivalent to circumcised men in this regard; and since women must study the laws of those commandments that are applicable to them, they have a share in the study of Torah.

11 / BLESSING AFTER MEALS

וְעַל הַכּל, יהוה אֱלֹהֵינוּ, אֲנַחְנוּ מוֹדִים לָךְ
For › everything, ‹‹ Hashem, ‹‹ our God, ‹‹ we › thank ‹ You ›

וּמְבָרְכִים אוֹתָךְ, יִתְבָּרַךְ שִׁמְךָ בְּפִי כָּל חַי
and bless › You. ‹ ‹‹ Blessed › may Your Name be ‹ by the mouth ‹ of all ‹ the living,

תָּמִיד לְעוֹלָם וָעֶד. כַּכָּתוּב, וְאָכַלְתָּ וְשָׂבָעְתָּ,
continuously › for ever ‹ and ever. ‹ ‹‹ As it is written: ‹‹ And you shall eat ‹ and you shall be satisfied

וּבֵרַכְתָּ אֶת יהוה אֱלֹהֶיךָ, עַל הָאָרֶץ הַטּבָה
and you shall bless ‹ Hashem, ‹ your God, ‹ for › the Land ‹ that is good

אֲשֶׁר נָתַן לָךְ.¹ ❖ בָּרוּךְ אַתָּה יהוה, עַל הָאָרֶץ
which › He gave ‹ you. ‹‹ Blessed › are You, ‹ Hashem, ‹‹ for › the Land

וְעַל הַמָּזוֹן. (אָמֵן. – *Others*)
and for › the nourishment. ‹‹ (Amen.) ‹‹

THIRD BLESSING: FOR JERUSALEM / בּוֹנֵה יְרוּשָׁלַיִם – הַבְּרָכָה הַשְּׁלִישִׁית

רַחֶם (נָא) יהוה אֱלֹהֵינוּ עַל יִשְׂרָאֵל עַמֶּךָ,
Have mercy, ‹ (we beg You) ‹ Hashem, ‹ our God, ‹‹ on › Israel ‹ Your people;‹‹

וְעַל יְרוּשָׁלַיִם עִירֶךָ, וְעַל צִיּוֹן מִשְׁכַּן כְּבוֹדֶךָ,
on › Jerusalem, ‹‹ Your City; ‹‹ on ‹ Zion, › the resting place ‹ of Your Glory;‹‹

---

(1) *Deuteronomy* 8:10.

בּוֹנֵה יְרוּשָׁלַיִם /
Third Blessing: For Jerusalem

This blessing is the final one required by the Torah. It was composed by David and Solomon. David, who conquered Jerusalem, referred to *Israel, Your people,* and *Jerusalem, Your City.* After the Temple was built, Solomon added, *the great and holy House* (*Berachos* 48b).

ఆ§ If One Forgot to Recite עַל הַנִּסִּים on Chanukah and Purim.

If one realized his error before reaching the Name Hashem at the end of this blessing (בָּרוּךְ אַתָּה ה', *Blessed are You, Hashem*) he should go back to עַל הַנִּסִּים and continue from there.

If he has already recited the phrase בָּרוּךְ אַתָּה ה', *Blessed are You, Hashem*, he continues to recite *Bircas HaMazon* until reaching the series of seasonal prayers which begin הָרַחֲמָן, *The compassionate One* (p. 20), and rectifies the omission as indicated there. If the omission is not discovered until after that point, nothing need be done.

וְעַל מַלְכוּת בֵּית דָּוִד מְשִׁיחֶךָ, וְעַל הַבַּיִת הַגָּדוֹל וְהַקָּדוֹשׁ שֶׁנִּקְרָא שִׁמְךָ עָלָיו. אֱלֹהֵינוּ אָבִינוּ, רְעֵנוּ זוּנֵנוּ פַּרְנְסֵנוּ וְכַלְכְּלֵנוּ וְהַרְוִיחֵנוּ, וְהַרְוַח לָנוּ יהוה אֱלֹהֵינוּ מְהֵרָה מִכָּל צָרוֹתֵינוּ. וְנָא אַל תַּצְרִיכֵנוּ יהוה אֱלֹהֵינוּ, לֹא לִידֵי מַתְּנַת בָּשָׂר וָדָם, וְלֹא לִידֵי הַלְוָאָתָם, כִּי אִם לְיָדְךָ הַמְּלֵאָה הַפְּתוּחָה הַקְּדוֹשָׁה וְהָרְחָבָה, שֶׁלֹּא נֵבוֹשׁ וְלֹא נִכָּלֵם לְעוֹלָם וָעֶד.

As composed by David and Solomon, the blessing was a prayer that God maintain the tranquility of the Land. Following the destruction and exile, the blessing was changed to embody a prayer for the return of the Land, the Temple, and the Davidic dynasty. Before David's conquest of Jerusalem, the blessing had yet another form (*Tur*), a request for God's mercy upon the nation (*Aruch HaShulchan*).

וְעַל מַלְכוּת בֵּית דָּוִד מְשִׁיחֶךָ — *On the monarchy of the house of David, Your anointed.* It is mandatory that the monarchy of David's dynasty be mentioned in this blessing. Whoever has not mentioned it has not fulfilled his obligation (*Berachos* 49a), because it was David who sanctified Jerusalem (*Rashi*), and because the consolation for the exile will not be complete until David's kingdom is restored (*Rambam*).

וְנָא אַל תַּצְרִיכֵנוּ . . . לִידֵי מַתְּנַת בָּשָׂר וָדָם — *Please, do not make us dependent . . . upon the gifts of flesh and blood,* do not make us dependent upon others. The firm believer knows that God's blessing will come inevitably without requiring him to beg for favors. However, if one feels compelled by the need to seek the help of others, his faith can be eroded. Thus we pray to God not to test us in this manner (*Olas Tamid*).

13 / BLESSING AFTER MEALS

ON THE SABBATH ADD THE FOLLOWING. [IF FORGOTTEN, SEE BELOW.]

רְצֵה וְהַחֲלִיצֵנוּ יהוה אֱלֹהֵינוּ בְּמִצְוֹתֶיךָ, וּבְמִצְוַת
May it be pleasing to You ⟨ to give us rest, ⟨ HASHEM, ⟨ our God, ⟨ through Your commandments ⟨ and through the commandment

יוֹם הַשְּׁבִיעִי הַשַּׁבָּת הַגָּדוֹל וְהַקָּדוֹשׁ הַזֶּה, כִּי יוֹם זֶה
of the Seventh Day, ⟨ that is great ⟨ and holy ⟨⟨ – this ⟨⟨ For, ⟨ this day,
the Sabbath one.

גָּדוֹל וְקָדוֹשׁ הוּא לְפָנֶיךָ, לִשְׁבָּת בּוֹ וְלָנוּחַ בּוֹ בְּאַהֲבָה
great ⟨ and holy ⟨ it is ⟨⟨ before You, ⟨⟨ to cease ⟨ on it ⟨ and to rest ⟨ on it, ⟨⟨ in love,

כְּמִצְוַת רְצוֹנֶךָ, וּבִרְצוֹנְךָ הָנִיחַ לָנוּ יהוה אֱלֹהֵינוּ,
as ordained ⟨ by Your will. ⟨⟨ And through Your will, ⟨ grant rest ⟨ to us, ⟨ HASHEM, ⟨⟨ our God,

שֶׁלֹּא תְהֵא צָרָה וְיָגוֹן וַאֲנָחָה בְּיוֹם מְנוּחָתֵנוּ, וְהַרְאֵנוּ
that there should not ⟨ be ⟨ any ⟨ grief, ⟨ or lament ⟨ on this day ⟨ of our rest. ⟨⟨ And show us,

יהוה אֱלֹהֵינוּ בְּנֶחָמַת צִיּוֹן עִירֶךָ, וּבְבִנְיַן יְרוּשָׁלַיִם
HASHEM, ⟨ our God, ⟨ the consolation ⟨ of Zion, ⟨ Your City, ⟨⟨ and the rebuilding ⟨ of Jerusalem,

עִיר קָדְשֶׁךָ, כִּי אַתָּה הוּא בַּעַל הַיְשׁוּעוֹת וּבַעַל הַנֶּחָמוֹת.
City ⟨ of Your holiness, ⟨ for ⟨ it is ⟨ You ⟨ Who are ⟨ Master ⟨ of salvations ⟨ and ⟨ Master ⟨⟨ of consolations.

⇜§ If One Omitted יַעֲלֶה וְיָבֹא or רְצֵה

(a) If he realizes his omission after having recited the blessing of בּוֹנֵה, *Who rebuilds,* he makes up for the omission by reciting the appropriate Compensatory Blessing (p. 22-23).

(b) If he realizes his omission after having recited the first six words of the fourth blessing, he may still switch immediately into the Compensatory Blessing since the words בָּרוּךְ אַתָּה ... הָעוֹלָם are identical in both blessings. (However, the Compensatory Blessing need not be recited after the third Sabbath meal if *Bircas HaMazon* is recited after sunset.)

(c) If the omission is discovered after having recited the word הָאֵל, *the Almighty,* of the fourth blessing, it is too late for the Compensatory Blessing to be recited. In that case:

(i) On the Sabbath and on a Festival day, at the first two meals *Bircas HaMazon* must be repeated in its entirety; at the third meal, nothing need be done.

(ii) On Rosh Chodesh and on Chol HaMoed, nothing need be done except if the day fell on the Sabbath and רְצֵה, *Retzei,* was omitted. In that case, at the first two meals *Bircas HaMazon* must be repeated. But if רְצֵה was recited and יַעֲלֶה וְיָבֹא was omitted, nothing need be done.

ON ROSH CHODESH, CHOL HAMOED, AND FESTIVALS ADD. [IF FORGOTTEN, SEE P. 13.]

אֱלֹהֵינוּ וֵאלֹהֵי אֲבוֹתֵינוּ, יַעֲלֶה, וְיָבֹא, וְיַגִּיעַ, וְיֵרָאֶה,
Our God 〈 and the 〈〈 of our 〈 may 〈〈 come, 〈 reach, 〈 be noted,
God forefathers, there rise,

וְיֵרָצֶה, וְיִשָּׁמַע, וְיִפָּקֵד, וְיִזָּכֵר זִכְרוֹנֵנוּ וּפִקְדוֹנֵנוּ, וְזִכְרוֹן
be 〈 be heard, 〈 be 〈〈 and be 〈 the — the 〈〈 and 〈 the
favored, considered, remembered remembrance consideration remem-
of us of us brance

אֲבוֹתֵינוּ, וְזִכְרוֹן מָשִׁיחַ בֶּן דָּוִד עַבְדֶּךָ, וְזִכְרוֹן יְרוּשָׁלַיִם
of our 〈〈 the 〈 of 〈 son 〈 Your 〈〈 the 〈 of Jerusalem,
forefathers; remembrance Messiah, of David, servant; remembrance

עִיר קָדְשֶׁךָ, וְזִכְרוֹן כָּל עַמְּךָ בֵּית יִשְׂרָאֵל לְפָנֶיךָ, לִפְלֵיטָה
City 〈 of Your 〈〈 holiness; 〈 remembrance 〈 of Your 〈 people 〈 entire 〈 Family 〈 of Israel — 〈 before 〈 You 〈〈 for deliverance,

לְטוֹבָה לְחֵן וּלְחֶסֶד וּלְרַחֲמִים, לְחַיִּים וּלְשָׁלוֹם, בְּיוֹם
for 〈 for 〈 for 〈 and for 〈 for 〈〈 and for 〈〈 on the
goodness, grace, kindness, compassion, life, peace, day of

ROSH CHODESH:	**PESACH:**	**SHAVUOS:**
רֹאשׁ הַחֹדֶשׁ	חַג הַמַּצּוֹת	חַג הַשָּׁבֻעוֹת
〈〈 that New 〈 Moon	〈〈 the Festival 〈 of Matzos	〈〈 the Festival 〈 of Shavuos

ROSH HASHANAH:	**SUCCOS:**	**SHEMINI ATZERES / SIMCHAS TORAH:**
הַזִּכָּרוֹן	חַג הַסֻּכּוֹת	הַשְּׁמִינִי חַג הָעֲצֶרֶת
〈〈 Remembrance	〈〈 the Festival 〈 of Succos	〈〈 the Shemini Atzeres Festival

הַזֶּה. זָכְרֵנוּ יהוה אֱלֹהֵינוּ בּוֹ לְטוֹבָה, וּפָקְדֵנוּ בוֹ לִבְרָכָה,
〈〈 — this. 〈 Remember 〈 Hashem, 〈 our God, 〈 on 〈 for 〈 consider 〈 on 〈 for
it goodness; us it blessing,

וְהוֹשִׁיעֵנוּ בוֹ לְחַיִּים. וּבִדְבַר יְשׁוּעָה וְרַחֲמִים, חוּס וְחָנֵּנוּ
and save us 〈 on it 〈 for life. 〈〈 In the 〈 of 〈 and 〈〈 have 〈 be
matter salvation compassion, pity, gracious

וְרַחֵם עָלֵינוּ וְהוֹשִׁיעֵנוּ, כִּי אֵלֶיךָ עֵינֵינוּ, כִּי אֵל
〈 and be com- 〈 with us, 〈〈 and save us, 〈 for 〈 to You 〈〈 are our 〈 because, 〈 God,
passionate eyes [turned],

(מֶלֶךְ) חַנּוּן וְרַחוּם אָתָּה.¹
〈 (King,) 〈 Who is 〈 and com- 〈 are You.
gracious passionate

---

(1) Cf. *Nechemiah* 9:31.

15 / BLESSING AFTER MEALS

❖ **וּבְנֵה** יְרוּשָׁלַיִם* עִיר הַקֹּדֶשׁ בִּמְהֵרָה בְיָמֵינוּ. בָּרוּךְ אַתָּה יהוה, בּוֹנֵה (בְּרַחֲמָיו) יְרוּשָׁלָיִם. אָמֵן.*

« Rebuild « Jerusalem,* « the City « of holiness, « soon « in our days. « Blessed « are You, « Hashem, « Who rebuilds «« (in His mercy) « Jerusalem. « Amen.* «« (Amen. – Others)

[WHEN REQUIRED, THE COMPENSATORY BLESSING (P. 22-23) IS RECITED HERE.]

FOURTH BLESSING: GOD'S GOODNESS / הברכה הרביעית – הטוב והמטיב

בָּרוּךְ אַתָּה יהוה אֱלֹהֵינוּ מֶלֶךְ הָעוֹלָם, הָאֵל אָבִינוּ מַלְכֵּנוּ אַדִּירֵנוּ בּוֹרְאֵנוּ גּוֹאֲלֵנוּ יוֹצְרֵנוּ קְדוֹשֵׁנוּ קְדוֹשׁ יַעֲקֹב, רוֹעֵנוּ רוֹעֵה יִשְׂרָאֵל, הַמֶּלֶךְ הַטּוֹב וְהַמֵּטִיב לַכֹּל, שֶׁבְּכָל יוֹם וָיוֹם* הוּא הֵטִיב, הוּא מֵטִיב, הוּא יֵיטִיב

« Blessed « are You, « Hashem, « our God, « King « of the universe, «« the Almighty, « our Father, « our King, « our Sovereign, « our Creator, « our Redeemer, « our Maker, « our Holy One, « Holy One « of Jacob, «« our Shepherd, « the Shepherd « of Israel, «« the King « Who is good « and Who does good « for all. « For, every «« day « after day* « He « did good, « He « does good, « and He « will do good

---

וּבְנֵה יְרוּשָׁלַיִם — *Rebuild Jerusalem.* This concludes the third blessing, and returns to the theme with which the blessing began — a plea for God's mercy on Jerusalem (*Pesachim* 104a).

אָמֵן — *Amen.* This blessing is unique in that one responds *Amen* after his own blessing. This unusual formula serves as a demarcation between the first three blessings which are ordained by the Torah and the next blessing which is Rabbinic in origin (*Berachos* 45b; *Rambam; Tur*). Since the word *Amen* is not part of the actual blessing, there should be a slight pause before it is said.

הַטּוֹב וְהַמֵּטִיב /
Fourth Blessing: For God's Goodness

The essence of this blessing is the phrase הַטּוֹב וְהַמֵּטִיב, *Who is good and Who does good.* The court of Rabban Gamliel the Elder in Yavneh composed this blessing in gratitude to God for preserving the bodies of the victims of the Roman massacre at Beitar, and for eventually allowing them to be brought to burial (*Berachos* 48b).

שֶׁבְּכָל יוֹם וָיוֹם — *For, every day after day.* It is insufficient to thank God for His graciousness to *past* generations. We must be conscious of the fact that His goodness and bounty occur constantly.

לָנוּ. הוּא גְמָלָנוּ הוּא גוֹמְלֵנוּ הוּא יִגְמְלֵנוּ
to us. » He « was bountiful » He « is bountiful » and He « will be bountiful with us, with us, with us,

לָעַד, לְחֵן וּלְחֶסֶד וּלְרַחֲמִים, וּלְרֶוַח הַצָּלָה
forever « with grace « and with kindness « and with compassion, « with relief, « rescue,

וְהַצְלָחָה, בְּרָכָה וִישׁוּעָה נֶחָמָה פַּרְנָסָה
« sustenance, « consolation, « salvation, « blessing, « success,

וְכַלְכָּלָה ❖ וְרַחֲמִים וְחַיִּים וְשָׁלוֹם וְכָל טוֹב,
« support, « compassion, « life, « peace, « and all good;

וּמִכָּל טוּב לְעוֹלָם אַל יְחַסְּרֵנוּ.* (אָמֵן – Others)
« and of all good things « may He forever « not « deprive us.* « (Amen.)

THE LEADER MAY PUT DOWN THE CUP OF WINE AT THIS POINT.

הָרַחֲמָן* הוּא יִמְלוֹךְ עָלֵינוּ לְעוֹלָם וָעֶד.
The compassionate One!* « May He « reign « over us « for ever « and ever.

הָרַחֲמָן הוּא יִתְבָּרַךְ בַּשָּׁמַיִם וּבָאָרֶץ. הָרַחֲמָן
« The compassionate One! « May He « be blessed « in heaven « and on earth. « The compassionate One!

הוּא יִשְׁתַּבַּח לְדוֹר דּוֹרִים, וְיִתְפָּאַר בָּנוּ
« May He « be praised « generation « after generation, « may He be glorified « through us

לָעַד וּלְנֵצַח נְצָחִים, וְיִתְהַדַּר בָּנוּ לָעַד
« forever « and to the ultimate time, « and be honored « through us « forever

וּלְעוֹלְמֵי עוֹלָמִים. הָרַחֲמָן הוּא יְפַרְנְסֵנוּ
« and for all eternity. « The compassionate One! « May He « sustain us

יְחַסְּרֵנוּ אַל לְעוֹלָם — *May He forever not deprive us.* This concludes the fourth blessing. Unlike the other blessings of *Bircas HaMazon*, this one does not conclude with a brief blessing summing up the theme of the section. As noted above, the essential text of the fourth blessing consists of the two words — הַטּוֹב וְהַמֵּטִיב, *Who is good and Who does good* — and it is therefore similar to the short blessings recited before performing a commandment or partaking of food. The addition to the text of considerable outpourings of gratitude does not alter the fact that the brief text does not require a double blessing (*Rashi* to *Berachos* 49a).

❧ **הָרַחֲמָן** — *The compassionate One!* After completing the four blessings of *Bircas HaMazon* we recite a selection of brief prayers for God's compassion (*Aruch HaShulchan*).

17 / BLESSING AFTER MEALS

בִּכָבוֹד. הָרַחֲמָן הוּא יִשְׁבּוֹר עֻלֵּנוּ מֵעַל צַוָּארֵנוּ,
in honor. The compassionate One! May He break our yoke [of oppression] from our necks,

וְהוּא יוֹלִיכֵנוּ קוֹמְמִיּוּת לְאַרְצֵנוּ. הָרַחֲמָן הוּא
and may He guide us erect to our Land. The compassionate One! May He

יִשְׁלַח לָנוּ בְּרָכָה מְרֻבָּה בַּבַּיִת הַזֶּה, וְעַל
send us blessing that is abundant to this house, and upon

שֻׁלְחָן זֶה שֶׁאָכַלְנוּ עָלָיו. הָרַחֲמָן הוּא יִשְׁלַח
this table that we have eaten on it. The compassionate One! May He send

לָנוּ אֶת אֵלִיָּהוּ הַנָּבִיא זָכוּר לַטּוֹב, וִיבַשֶּׂר
us Elijah the Prophet — who is remembered for good — to proclaim

לָנוּ* בְּשׂוֹרוֹת טוֹבוֹת יְשׁוּעוֹת וְנֶחָמוֹת.
to us* tidings that are good, salvations, and consolations.

THE FOLLOWING IS A BLESSING THAT A GUEST RECITES FOR HIS HOST.

יְהִי רָצוֹן שֶׁלֹּא יֵבוֹשׁ וְלֹא יִכָּלֵם בַּעַל הַבַּיִת הַזֶּה,
May it be that [God's] will that he not be ashamed nor be humiliated — the master of this house —

לֹא בָּעוֹלָם הַזֶּה וְלֹא בָּעוֹלָם הַבָּא, וְיַצְלִיחַ בְּכָל
not in This World nor in the World to Come. May he be successful in all

נְכָסָיו,* וְיִהְיוּ נְכָסָיו מַצְלִיחִים וּקְרוֹבִים לָעִיר,* וְאַל
his dealings.* May his dealings be successful and [conveniently] close at hand.* May there not

יִשְׁלוֹט שָׂטָן בְּמַעֲשֵׂה יָדָיו, וְאַל יִזְדַּקֵּק לְפָנָיו שׁוּם
be in control any evil impediment over the work of his hands, and may there not attach to him itself any

דְּבַר חֵטְא וְהִרְהוּר עָוֹן, מֵעַתָּה וְעַד עוֹלָם.
matter of transgression or thought of sin, from this time until eternity.

וִיבַשֶּׂר לָנוּ — *To proclaim to us.* Elijah will proclaim the news of the arrival of Messiah [Malachi 3:23] (*Iyun Tefillah*).

נְכָסָיו — *His dealings.* Lit. *his possessions.*

וּקְרוֹבִים לָעִיר — *And close at hand.* Lit. *and close to the city.*

GUESTS RECITE THE FOLLOWING (CHILDREN AT THEIR PARENTS' TABLE INCLUDE THE APPLICABLE WORDS IN PARENTHESES):

הָרַחֲמָן הוּא יְבָרֵךְ
The compassionate One! ⟨ May He ⟨ bless ⟩

אֶת (אָבִי מוֹרִי) בַּעַל הַבַּיִת הַזֶּה,
⟨ my father, ⟨ my teacher) ⟨ the master ⟨ of this house, ⟩

וְאֶת (אִמִּי מוֹרָתִי) בַּעֲלַת הַבַּיִת הַזֶּה,
and ⟨ ⟨my mother, ⟨ my teacher) ⟨ the lady ⟨ of this house ⟩⟩

אוֹתָם וְאֶת בֵּיתָם וְאֶת זַרְעָם וְאֶת כָּל אֲשֶׁר לָהֶם.
⟨ — them, ⟨ their house, ⟨ and ⟨ their family, ⟨ and ⟨ all ⟨ that ⟩⟩ is theirs. ⟩

AT ONE'S OWN TABLE (INCLUDE THE APPLICABLE WORDS IN PARENTHESES):

הָרַחֲמָן הוּא יְבָרֵךְ אוֹתִי
The compassionate One! ⟨ May He ⟨ bless ⟨ me ⟩

(וְאֶת אִשְׁתִּי / וְאֶת בַּעֲלִי. וְאֶת זַרְעִי
(⟨ and ⟨ my wife ⟨ / ⟨ my husband ⟨ and ⟨ my children ⟩

וְאֶת כָּל אֲשֶׁר לִי.
and ⟨ all ⟨ that ⟨ is mine. ⟩⟩

ALL CONTINUE:

אוֹתָנוּ וְאֶת כָּל אֲשֶׁר לָנוּ, כְּמוֹ שֶׁנִּתְבָּרְכוּ
⟨ Us ⟨ and ⟨ all ⟨ that ⟨ is ours ⟩⟩ — just as ⟨ blessed were ⟩

אֲבוֹתֵינוּ אַבְרָהָם יִצְחָק וְיַעֲקֹב בַּכֹּל מִכֹּל
⟨ our forefathers, ⟨ Abraham, ⟨ Isaac, ⟨ and Jacob — ⟩⟩ in everything, from everything,

כֹּל,*¹ כֵּן יְבָרֵךְ אוֹתָנוּ כֻּלָּנוּ יַחַד בִּבְרָכָה
with everything.* ⟨ So ⟨ may He bless ⟨ us, ⟨ all of us, ⟨ together, ⟨ with a blessing ⟩

שְׁלֵמָה, וְנֹאמַר, אָמֵן.
⟨ that is perfect. ⟨ And let us say: ⟨ Amen! ⟩⟩

---

(1) Cf. *Genesis* 24:1; 27:33; 33:11.

בַּכֹּל מִכֹּל כֹּל — *In everything, from everything, with everything.* The three expressions, each indicating that no necessary measure of goodness was lacking, are used by the Torah referring respectively to the three Patriarchs.

19 / BLESSING AFTER MEALS

בַּמָּרוֹם יְלַמְּדוּ עֲלֵיהֶם* וְעָלֵינוּ* זְכוּת,
‹ On high, ›‹ may there be pleaded ›‹ upon them* ›‹ and upon us,* ›‹ merit ›

שֶׁתְּהֵא לְמִשְׁמֶרֶת שָׁלוֹם.* וְנִשָּׂא בְרָכָה
‹ that may serve ›‹ for a safeguard ›‹ of peace.* ›‹ May we receive ›‹ a blessing ›

מֵאֵת יהוה, וּצְדָקָה מֵאֱלֹהֵי יִשְׁעֵנוּ, וְנִמְצָא
‹ from Hashem, ›‹ and kindness that is just ›‹ from the God ›‹ of our salvation, ›‹ and may we find ›

חֵן וְשֵׂכֶל טוֹב בְּעֵינֵי אֱלֹהִים וְאָדָם.¹
‹ favor ›‹ and good understanding ›‹ in the eyes ›‹ of God ›‹ and man. ›

AT A CIRCUMCISION FEAST CONTINUE WITH הָרַחֲמָן, *THE COMPASSIONATE ONE*, P. 31.

IF ANY OF THE FOLLOWING VERSES WAS OMITTED, *BIRCAS HAMAZON* **NEED NOT BE REPEATED.**

ON THE SABBATH ADD:

הָרַחֲמָן הוּא יַנְחִילֵנוּ יוֹם שֶׁכֻּלּוֹ שַׁבָּת*
‹ The compassionate One! ›‹ May He ›‹ cause us to inherit ›‹ the day ›‹ which will be completely ›‹ a Sabbath* ›

וּמְנוּחָה לְחַיֵּי הָעוֹלָמִים.
‹ and a rest day ›‹ for life ›‹ that is eternal. ›

ON ROSH CHODESH ADD:

הָרַחֲמָן הוּא יְחַדֵּשׁ עָלֵינוּ אֶת הַחֹדֶשׁ הַזֶּה לְטוֹבָה וְלִבְרָכָה.
‹ The compassionate One! ›‹ May He ›‹ inaugurate ›‹ upon us ›‹ this month ›‹ for goodness ›‹ and for blessing. ›

ON FESTIVALS ADD:

הָרַחֲמָן הוּא יַנְחִילֵנוּ יוֹם שֶׁכֻּלּוֹ טוֹב.
‹ The compassionate One! ›‹ May He ›‹ cause us to inherit ›‹ the day ›‹ which is completely ›‹ good. ›

ON ROSH HASHANAH ADD:

הָרַחֲמָן הוּא יְחַדֵּשׁ עָלֵינוּ אֶת הַשָּׁנָה הַזֹּאת לְטוֹבָה וְלִבְרָכָה.
‹ The compassionate One! ›‹ May He ›‹ inaugurate ›‹ upon us ›‹ this year ›‹ for goodness ›‹ and for blessing. ›

---

(1) Cf. *Proverbs* 3:4.

עֲלֵיהֶם — *Upon them,* the master and mistress of the home, or any others who were mentioned in the preceding prayer.

וְעָלֵינוּ — *And upon us,* all gathered around the table. [When one eats alone this term refers to the people who were previously specified and to the Jewish people in general.]

לְמִשְׁמֶרֶת שָׁלוֹם — *For a safeguard of peace,* to assure that the home will be peaceful.

יוֹם שֶׁכֻּלּוֹ שַׁבָּת — *The day which will be completely a Sabbath,* an allusion to the World to Come after the final Redemption.

ברכת המזון / 20

ON SUCCOS ADD:

הָרַחֲמָן הוּא יָקִים לָנוּ אֶת סֻכַּת דָּוִיד הַנֹּפֶלֶת.[1]
《 which is fallen. 〈 of David, 〈 the booth 〈 for us 〈 erect 〈 May He 〈 The compassionate One!

ON CHANUKAH AND PURIM, IF AL HANISSIM WAS NOT RECITED IN ITS PROPER PLACE, ADD:

הָרַחֲמָן הוּא יַעֲשֶׂה לָנוּ נִסִּים וְנִפְלָאוֹת
〈 and wonders 〈 miracles 〈 for us 〈 perform 〈 May He 〈 The compassionate One!

כַּאֲשֶׁר עָשָׂה לַאֲבוֹתֵינוּ בַּיָּמִים הָהֵם בַּזְּמַן הַזֶּה.
《 at this time. 〈 in those days, 〈 for our forefathers 〈 He performed 〈 as

ON CHANUKAH CONTINUE בִּימֵי — *IN THE DAYS OF* . . . (P. 9).
ON PURIM CONTINUE בִּימֵי — *IN THE DAYS OF* . . . (P. 10).

הָרַחֲמָן הוּא יְזַכֵּנוּ לִימוֹת הַמָּשִׁיחַ וּלְחַיֵּי
〈 and of the life 〈 of Messiah 〈 of the days 〈 make us worthy 〈 May He 〈 The compassionate One!

DAYS *MUSSAF* IS RECITED:	WEEKDAYS:

מִגְדּוֹל*] יְשׁוּעוֹת מַלְכּוֹ   [מַגְדִּיל* הָעוֹלָם הַבָּא.
〈 to His king 〈 salvations 〈 He Who is a tower* of   He Who magnifies* 《 to Come. 〈 of the World

וְעֹשֶׂה חֶסֶד לִמְשִׁיחוֹ לְדָוִד וּלְזַרְעוֹ עַד עוֹלָם.[2]
《 forever. 〈 and to his offspring 〈 to David 〈 to His anointed, 〈 kindness 〈 and does

עֹשֶׂה שָׁלוֹם בִּמְרוֹמָיו,*[3] הוּא יַעֲשֶׂה שָׁלוֹם עָלֵינוּ
《 upon us 〈 peace 〈 make 〈 may He 〈 in His heights,* 〈 peace 〈 He Who makes

וְעַל כָּל יִשְׂרָאֵל.[4] וְאִמְרוּ, אָמֵן.
《 Amen! 〈 Now respond: 《 Israel. 〈 all 〈 and upon

---

(1) Cf. *Amos* 9:11. (2) *Psalms* 18:51, *II Samuel* 22:51. (3) *Job* 25:2. (4) Cf. *Berachos* 16b.

מַגְדִּיל/מִגְדּוֹל — *He Who magnifies/is a tower.* Both verses were written by King David and, in the context of *Bircas HaMazon*, *king* refers to King Messiah. The phrase from *Psalms* [מַגְדִּיל] was chosen for weekdays because it was written before David became king. David composed the phrase from *Samuel* [מִגְדּוֹל] when he was at the peak of his greatness, and it is therefore more suited to the Sabbath and Festivals (*Etz Yosef*).

עֹשֶׂה שָׁלוֹם בִּמְרוֹמָיו — *He Who makes peace in His heights.* Even the heavenly beings require God to make peace among them, how much more so fractious man! (*Etz Yosef*).

BLESSING AFTER MEALS

יְראוּ אֶת יהוה* קְדֹשָׁיו, כִּי אֵין מַחְסוֹר לִירֵאָיו. כְּפִירִים רָשׁוּ וְרָעֵבוּ, וְדֹרְשֵׁי יהוה לֹא יַחְסְרוּ כָל טוֹב.¹ הוֹדוּ לַיהוה כִּי טוֹב, כִּי לְעוֹלָם חַסְדּוֹ.² פּוֹתֵחַ אֶת יָדֶךָ, וּמַשְׂבִּיעַ לְכָל חַי רָצוֹן.³ בָּרוּךְ הַגֶּבֶר אֲשֶׁר יִבְטַח בַּיהוה, וְהָיָה יהוה מִבְטַחוֹ.⁴* נַעַר הָיִיתִי גַּם זָקַנְתִּי, וְלֹא רָאִיתִי צַדִּיק נֶעֱזָב, וְזַרְעוֹ מְבַקֶּשׁ לָחֶם.⁵* יהוה עֹז לְעַמּוֹ יִתֵּן, יהוה יְבָרֵךְ אֶת עַמּוֹ בַשָּׁלוֹם.⁶*

Fear Hashem, O [you] His holy ones, for there is no deprivation for His reverent ones. Young lions may want and hunger, but those who seek Hashem will not lack any good. Give thanks to Hashem, for He is good, for His kindness is enduring forever. You open Your hand, and satisfy every living thing [with its] desire. Blessed is the man who trusts in Hashem; then Hashem will be his security.* A youth I have been and also I have aged; but I have not seen a righteous man forsaken, nor his children begging for bread.* Hashem will give strength to His people, Hashem will bless His people with peace.*

---

(1) *Psalms* 34:10-11. (2) 136:1 et al. (3) 145:16. (4) *Jeremiah* 17:7. (5) *Psalms* 37:25. (6) 29:11.

יְראוּ אֶת ה׳ — *Fear Hashem.* Those who fear God are content, even if they are lacking in material possessions. But the wicked are never satisfied; whatever they have only whets their appetite for more (*Anaf Yosef*).

אֲשֶׁר יִבְטַח בַּה׳ וְהָיָה ה׳ מִבְטַחוֹ — *Who trusts in Hashem; then Hashem will be his security.* God will be a bastion of trust to a man in direct proportion to the amount of trust he places in God (*Chidushei HaRim*).

צַדִּיק נֶעֱזָב וְזַרְעוֹ מְבַקֶּשׁ לָחֶם — *A righteous man forsaken, nor his children begging for bread.* A righteous man may suffer misfortune, but God will surely have mercy on His children (*Radak; Malbim*). I have never seen a righteous man consider himself forsaken even if his children must beg for bread. Whatever his lot in life, he trusts that God brings it upon him for a constructive and merciful purpose (*Anaf Yosef*).

בְּשָׁלוֹם — *With peace.* Rabbi Shimon ben Chalafta said: "The Holy One, Blessed is He, could find no container which would hold Israel's blessings as well as peace would, as it says: *Hashem to His people will give strength, Hashem will bless His people with peace*" (*Uktzin* 3:12).

⊰ COMPENSATORY BLESSINGS / ברכות למי ששכח ⊱

SEE BELOW AND ON PAGE 13 FOR INSTANCES WHEN COMPENSATORY BLESSINGS MUST BE RECITED. WHEN THE COMPENSATORY BLESSING IS RECITED AT THE FIRST OR SECOND SABBATH OR FESTIVAL MEAL, ONE CONCLUDES WITH ... בָּרוּךְ אַתָּה ה' מְקַדֵּשׁ. AT THE THIRD MEAL THIS CLOSING BLESSING IS NOT RECITED. AFTER THE APPROPRIATE BLESSING, CONTINUE WITH THE FOURTH BLESSING, GOD'S GOODNESS (P. 15).

IF ONE FORGOT רְצֵה ON THE SABBATH:

בָּרוּךְ אַתָּה יהוה אֱלֹהֵינוּ מֶלֶךְ הָעוֹלָם, אֲשֶׁר נָתַן שַׁבָּתוֹת
〈 Sabbaths 〈 gave 〈 Who 〈〈 of the universe, 〈 King 〈 our God, 〈 Hashem, 〈 are You, 〈 Blessed

לִמְנוּחָה לְעַמּוֹ יִשְׂרָאֵל בְּאַהֲבָה, לְאוֹת וְלִבְרִית. בָּרוּךְ אַתָּה
〈 are You, 〈 Blessed 〈〈 and for a covenant. 〈 for a sign 〈 with love, 〈 Israel 〈 to His people 〈 for rest

יהוה, מְקַדֵּשׁ הַשַּׁבָּת.
〈〈 the Sabbath. 〈 Who sanctifies 〈 Hashem,

IF ONE FORGOT יַעֲלֶה וְיָבֹא ON ROSH CHODESH:

בָּרוּךְ אַתָּה יהוה אֱלֹהֵינוּ מֶלֶךְ הָעוֹלָם, אֲשֶׁר נָתַן רָאשֵׁי חֳדָשִׁים
〈 Moons 〈 New 〈 gave 〈 Who 〈〈 of the universe, 〈 King 〈 our God, 〈 Hashem, 〈 are You, 〈 Blessed

לְעַמּוֹ יִשְׂרָאֵל לְזִכָּרוֹן.
〈〈 as a remembrance. 〈 Israel 〈 to His people

IF ONE FORGOT BOTH רְצֵה AND יַעֲלֶה וְיָבֹא ON ROSH CHODESH THAT FALLS ON THE SABBATH:

בָּרוּךְ אַתָּה יהוה אֱלֹהֵינוּ מֶלֶךְ הָעוֹלָם, אֲשֶׁר נָתַן שַׁבָּתוֹת
〈 Sabbaths 〈 gave 〈 Who 〈〈 of the universe, 〈 King 〈 our God, 〈 Hashem, 〈 are You, 〈 Blessed

לִמְנוּחָה לְעַמּוֹ יִשְׂרָאֵל בְּאַהֲבָה, לְאוֹת וְלִבְרִית, וְרָאשֵׁי חֳדָשִׁים
〈 Moons 〈 and New 〈〈 and for a covenant, 〈 for a sign 〈〈 with love, 〈 Israel 〈 to His people 〈 for rest

לְזִכָּרוֹן. בָּרוּךְ אַתָּה יהוה, מְקַדֵּשׁ הַשַּׁבָּת וְיִשְׂרָאֵל וְרָאשֵׁי חֳדָשִׁים.
〈〈 Moons. 〈 and New 〈 Israel, 〈 the Sabbath, 〈 Who sanctifies 〈 Hashem, 〈 are 〈 Blessed 〈〈 for a re-
                                                                                                         You,   membrance.

IF ONE FORGOT יַעֲלֶה וְיָבֹא ON A FESTIVAL:

בָּרוּךְ אַתָּה יהוה אֱלֹהֵינוּ מֶלֶךְ הָעוֹלָם, אֲשֶׁר נָתַן יָמִים טוֹבִים
〈 Festivals 〈 gave 〈 Who 〈〈 of the universe, 〈 King 〈 our God, 〈 Hashem, 〈 are You, 〈 Blessed

לְעַמּוֹ יִשְׂרָאֵל לְשָׂשׂוֹן וּלְשִׂמְחָה, אֶת יוֹם
〈 – the day of [the] 〈〈 and gladness 〈 for happiness 〈 Israel 〈 to His people

SHEMINI ATZERES/SIMCHAS TORAH	SUCCOS	SHAVUOS	PESACH
הַשְּׁמִינִי חַג הָעֲצֶרֶת	חַג הַסֻּכּוֹת	חַג הַשָּׁבֻעוֹת	חַג הַמַּצּוֹת
〈〈 Festival of Shemini Atzeres	〈〈Festival of Succos	〈〈 Festival of Shavuos	〈〈Festival of Matzos

הַזֶּה. בָּרוּךְ אַתָּה יהוה, מְקַדֵּשׁ יִשְׂרָאֵל וְהַזְּמַנִּים.
〈〈 and the [festive] seasons. 〈 Israel 〈 Who sanctifies 〈 Hashem, 〈 are You, 〈 Blessed 〈〈 – this.

23 / BLESSING AFTER MEALS — COMPENSATORY BLESSINGS

IF ONE FORGOT BOTH רְצֵה AND יַעֲלֶה וְיָבֹא ON A FESTIVAL THAT FALLS ON THE SABBATH:

בָּרוּךְ אַתָּה יהוה אֱלֹהֵינוּ מֶלֶךְ הָעוֹלָם, אֲשֶׁר נָתַן שַׁבָּתוֹת
Blessed ⟩ are You, ⟨ Hashem, ⟩ our God, ⟨ King ⟩ of the universe, ⟨ Who ⟩ gave ⟨ Sabbaths ⟩

לִמְנוּחָה לְעַמּוֹ יִשְׂרָאֵל בְּאַהֲבָה, לְאוֹת וְלִבְרִית, וְיָמִים טוֹבִים
for rest ⟩ to His people ⟨ Israel ⟩ with love, ⟨⟨ for a sign ⟩ and a covenant, ⟨ and Festivals ⟩

לְשָׂשׂוֹן וּלְשִׂמְחָה, אֶת יוֹם
for happiness ⟩ and gladness ⟨⟨ — the day of [the] ⟩

SHEMINI ATZERES/SIMCHAS TORAH	SUCCOS	SHAVUOS	PESACH
הַשְּׁמִינִי חַג הָעֲצֶרֶת	חַג הַסֻּכּוֹת	חַג הַשָּׁבֻעוֹת	חַג הַמַּצוֹת
⟨⟨ Festival of Shemini Atzeres	⟨⟨Festival of Succos	⟨⟨ Festival of Shavuos	⟨⟨Festival of Matzos

הַזֶּה. בָּרוּךְ אַתָּה יהוה, מְקַדֵּשׁ הַשַּׁבָּת וְיִשְׂרָאֵל וְהַזְּמַנִּים.
⟨⟨— this. ⟩ Blessed ⟨ are You, ⟩ Hashem, ⟨ Who sanctifies ⟩ the Sabbath, ⟨ Israel, ⟩ and the [festive] seasons.

IF ONE FORGOT יַעֲלֶה וְיָבֹא ON CHOL HAMOED:

בָּרוּךְ אַתָּה יהוה אֱלֹהֵינוּ מֶלֶךְ הָעוֹלָם, אֲשֶׁר נָתַן מוֹעֲדִים לְעַמּוֹ
Blessed ⟩ are You, ⟨ Hashem, ⟩ our God, ⟨ King ⟩ of the universe, ⟨⟨ Who ⟩ gave ⟨ appointed Festivals ⟩ to His people ⟨

יִשְׂרָאֵל לְשָׂשׂוֹן וּלְשִׂמְחָה, אֶת יוֹם
Israel ⟩ for happiness ⟨ and gladness ⟨⟨ — the day of ⟩

ON SUCCOS:	ON PESACH:
חַג הַסֻּכּוֹת הַזֶּה.	חַג הַמַּצוֹת הַזֶּה.
⟨⟨ this Festival of Succos.	⟨⟨ this Festival of Matzos.

IF ONE FORGOT BOTH רְצֵה AND יַעֲלֶה וְיָבֹא ON THE SABBATH OF CHOL HAMOED:

בָּרוּךְ אַתָּה יהוה אֱלֹהֵינוּ מֶלֶךְ הָעוֹלָם, אֲשֶׁר נָתַן שַׁבָּתוֹת
Blessed ⟩ are You, ⟨ Hashem, ⟩ our God, ⟨ King ⟩ of the universe, ⟨ Who ⟩ gave ⟨ Sabbaths ⟩

לִמְנוּחָה לְעַמּוֹ יִשְׂרָאֵל בְּאַהֲבָה, לְאוֹת וְלִבְרִית, וּמוֹעֲדִים לְשָׂשׂוֹן
for rest ⟩ to His people ⟨ Israel ⟩ with love, ⟨⟨ for a sign ⟩ and a covenant, ⟨ and appointed Festivals ⟩ for happiness

וּלְשִׂמְחָה, אֶת יוֹם
and gladness ⟨⟨ — the day of ⟩

ON SUCCOS:	ON PESACH:
חַג הַסֻּכּוֹת הַזֶּה.	חַג הַמַּצוֹת הַזֶּה.
⟨⟨ this Festival of Succos.	⟨⟨ this Festival of Matzos.

בָּרוּךְ אַתָּה יהוה, מְקַדֵּשׁ הַשַּׁבָּת וְיִשְׂרָאֵל וְהַזְּמַנִּים.
Blessed ⟩ are You, ⟨ Hashem, ⟩ Who sanctifies ⟨⟨ the Sabbath, ⟩ Israel, ⟨ and the [festive] seasons. ⟨⟨

BLESSINGS AFTER OTHER FOODS / ברכות אחרונות
THE THREE-FACETED BLESSING / מעין שלש

THE FOLLOWING BLESSING IS RECITED AFTER PARTAKING OF: (A) GRAIN PRODUCTS (OTHER THAN BREAD OR MATZAH) MADE FROM WHEAT, BARLEY, RYE, OATS, OR SPELT; (B) GRAPE WINE OR GRAPE JUICE; (C) GRAPES, FIGS, POMEGRANATES, OLIVES, OR DATES. (IF FOODS FROM TWO OR THREE OF THESE GROUPS WERE EATEN, THEN THE INSERTIONS FOR EACH GROUP ARE CONNECTED WITH THE CONJUNCTIVE ן, THUS וְעַל. THE ORDER IN SUCH A CASE IS GRAIN, WINE, FRUIT.)

בָּרוּךְ אַתָּה יהוה אֱלֹהֵינוּ מֶלֶךְ הָעוֹלָם, עַל
Blessed ⟩ are You, ⟨⟨ Hashem, ⟨⟨ our God, ⟩ King ⟨ of the universe, ⟨⟨ for ⟩

AFTER GRAIN PRODUCTS:
הַמִּחְיָה וְעַל
⟨ and for ⟨ the nourishment
הַכַּלְכָּלָה,
⟨ the sustenance

AFTER WINE:
[וְעַל] הַגֶּפֶן וְעַל
⟨ and for ⟩ the vine ⟨ [and for]
פְּרִי הַגֶּפֶן,
⟨ the fruit ⟨ of the vine,

AFTER FRUITS:
[וְעַל] הָעֵץ וְעַל
⟨ and for ⟨ the tree ⟨ [and for]
פְּרִי הָעֵץ,
⟨ the fruit ⟨ of the tree,

וְעַל תְּנוּבַת הַשָּׂדֶה, וְעַל אֶרֶץ חֶמְדָּה טוֹבָה וּרְחָבָה,
and for ⟨ the produce ⟨ of the field; ⟨⟨ for ⟨ the Land ⟨ – desirable, ⟨ good, ⟨⟨ and spacious –

שֶׁרָצִיתָ וְהִנְחַלְתָּ לַאֲבוֹתֵינוּ, לֶאֱכוֹל מִפִּרְיָהּ וְלִשְׂבּוֹעַ מִטּוּבָהּ.
that You ⟩ desired ⟨ and gave as ⟨ to our ⟨⟨ to eat ⟨ of its fruit ⟨ and to ⟨⟨ with its
a heritage forefathers, be satisfied goodness.

רַחֵם (נָא) יהוה אֱלֹהֵינוּ עַל יִשְׂרָאֵל עַמֶּךָ, וְעַל
Have mercy, ⟩ (we beg You,) ⟨⟨ Hashem, ⟨⟨ our God, ⟩ on ⟨ Israel ⟨ Your people; ⟨ on

יְרוּשָׁלַיִם עִירֶךָ, וְעַל צִיּוֹן מִשְׁכַּן כְּבוֹדֶךָ, וְעַל מִזְבְּחֶךָ
Jerusalem, ⟩ Your City; ⟨ on ⟨ Zion ⟨ the resting place ⟨⟨ of Your glory; ⟨ on ⟨⟨ Your Altar,

וְעַל הֵיכָלֶךָ. וּבְנֵה יְרוּשָׁלַיִם עִיר הַקֹּדֶשׁ בִּמְהֵרָה בְיָמֵינוּ,
and on ⟨ Your Temple. ⟨⟨ Rebuild ⟨ Jerusalem, the City ⟨ of holiness, ⟨ speedily ⟨⟨ in our days.

וְהַעֲלֵנוּ לְתוֹכָהּ, וְשַׂמְּחֵנוּ בְּבִנְיָנָהּ, וְנֹאכַל מִפִּרְיָהּ, וְנִשְׂבַּע
Bring us up ⟩ into it ⟨ and gladden ⟨⟨ in its ⟨ let us eat ⟨⟨ from its ⟨ and let us
us rebuilding; fruit be satisfied

מִטּוּבָהּ, וּנְבָרֶכְךָ עָלֶיהָ בִּקְדֻשָּׁה וּבְטָהֳרָה.
⟨⟨ with its goodness, ⟨ and let us bless You ⟨ upon it ⟨ in holiness ⟨⟨ and purity.

ON THE SABBATH:
רְצֵה וְהַחֲלִיצֵנוּ בְּיוֹם הַשַּׁבָּת הַזֶּה.
And may it be pleasing to You ⟩ to give us rest ⟨ on this Sabbath day. ⟨⟨

ON ROSH CHODESH:
וְזָכְרֵנוּ (לְטוֹבָה) בְּיוֹם רֹאשׁ הַחֹדֶשׁ הַזֶּה.
And remember us ⟩ (for goodness) ⟨ on the day ⟨ of this New Moon. ⟨⟨

ON PESACH:
וְשַׂמְּחֵנוּ בְּיוֹם חַג הַמַּצּוֹת הַזֶּה.
And gladden us ⟩ on the day ⟨ of this Festival of Matzos.

BLESSINGS AFTER OTHER FOODS

ON SHAVUOS:
וְשַׂמְּחֵנוּ בְּיוֹם חַג הַשָּׁבֻעוֹת הַזֶּה.
≪ of this Festival of Shavuos. ≪ on the day ≪ And gladden us

ON ROSH HASHANAH:
וְזָכְרֵנוּ (לְטוֹבָה) בְּיוֹם הַזִּכָּרוֹן הַזֶּה.
≪ on this Day of Remembrance. ≪ (for goodness) ≪ And remember us

ON SUCCOS:
וְשַׂמְּחֵנוּ בְּיוֹם חַג הַסֻּכּוֹת הַזֶּה.
≪ of this Festival of Succos. ≪ on the day ≪ And gladden us

ON SHEMINI ATZERES / SIMCHAS TORAH:
וְשַׂמְּחֵנוּ בְּיוֹם הַשְּׁמִינִי חַג הָעֲצֶרֶת הַזֶּה.
≪ of this Festival of Shemini Atzeres. ≪ on the day ≪ And gladden us

כִּי אַתָּה יהוה טוֹב וּמֵטִיב לַכֹּל, וְנוֹדֶה לְּךָ עַל הָאָרֶץ וְעַל
≪ and ≪ the Land ≪ for You ≪ and we ≪ to all, ≪ and do ≪ are ≪ Hashem, ≪ You, ≪ For
for thank good good

| **AFTER FRUITS:** | **AFTER WINE:** | **AFTER GRAIN PRODUCTS:** |

[וְעַל] הַפֵּרוֹת.°° [וְעַל] פְּרִי הַגֶּפֶן.° הַמִּחְיָה (וְעַל הַכַּלְכָּלָה).
≪ the fruit. ≪ [and ≪ of the ≪ the ≪ [and ≪ the ≪ (and ≪ the
for] vine. fruit for] sustenance). for nourishment

בָּרוּךְ אַתָּה יהוה, עַל הָאָרֶץ וְעַל
≪ and for ≪ the Land ≪ for ≪ Hashem, ≪ are You, ≪ Blessed

[וְעַל] הַפֵּרוֹת.°° [וְעַל] פְּרִי הַגֶּפֶן.° הַמִּחְיָה (וְעַל הַכַּלְכָּלָה).
≪ the fruit. ≪ [and ≪ of the ≪ the ≪ [and ≪ the ≪ (and ≪ the
for] vine. fruit for] sustenance). for nourishment

°°**ON WINE FROM** *ERETZ YISRAEL*, **SUBSTITUTE** גַּפְנָהּ, *OF ITS VINE,* **FOR** הַגֶּפֶן, *OF THE VINE.*
°°**ON FRUIT FROM** *ERETZ YISRAEL*, **SUBSTITUTE** פֵּרוֹתֶיהָ, *ITS FRUIT,* **FOR** הַפֵּרוֹת, *THE FRUIT.*

BOREI NEFASHOS / בורא נפשות

AFTER ANY FOOD TO WHICH NEITHER BIRCAS HAMAZON NOR THE THREE-FACETED BLESSING APPLIES,
SUCH AS FRUITS OTHER THAN THE ABOVE, VEGETABLES, OR BEVERAGES OTHER THAN WINE, RECITE:

בָּרוּךְ אַתָּה יהוה אֱלֹהֵינוּ מֶלֶךְ הָעוֹלָם, בּוֹרֵא נְפָשׁוֹת רַבּוֹת
≪ numerous ≪ Who ≪ of the ≪ King ≪ our God, ≪ Hashem, ≪ are You, ≪ Blessed
living things creates universe,

וְחֶסְרוֹנָן, עַל כָּל מַה שֶּׁבָּרָא (שֶׁבָּרָאתָ – SOME SUBSTITUTE) לְהַחֲיוֹת בָּהֶם
≪ with which to ≪ (You have ≪ He has ≪ that ≪ all ≪ for ≪ with their
sustain created) created deficiencies;

נֶפֶשׁ כָּל חָי. בָּרוּךְ חֵי הָעוֹלָמִים.
≪ of the ≪ the ≪ Blessed ≪ being. ≪ of ≪ the life
worlds. Life-giver is He, every

---

(1) When the blessing includes fruit, say הַגֶּפֶן.

✺{ SHEVA BERACHOS / שֶׁבַע בְּרָכוֹת }✺

WHEN SHEVA BERACHOS ARE RECITED, THE LEADER RECITES THE FOLLOWING ZIMUN, WITH A CUP OF WINE IN HAND.

Leader – רַבּוֹתַי מִיר וֶועלֶען בֶּענְטשֶׁען [רַבּוֹתַי נְבָרֵךְ].
》 [let us bless. 〈 Gentlemen,] 》 bless. 〈 let us 〈 Gentlemen,

Others – יְהִי שֵׁם יהוה מְבֹרָךְ מֵעַתָּה וְעַד עוֹלָם.[1]
》 eternity. 〈 until 〈 from 〈 be 〈 of 〈 the 〈 Let
this time blessed HASHEM Name

Leader – יְהִי שֵׁם יהוה מְבֹרָךְ מֵעַתָּה וְעַד עוֹלָם.[1]
》 eternity. 〈 until 〈 from 〈 be 〈 of 〈 the 〈 Let
this time blessed HASHEM Name

IN MANY CONGREGATIONS THE FOLLOWING IS NOT RECITED ON THE SABBATH:

Leader – דְּוַי הָסֵר וְגַם חָרוֹן, וְאָז אִלֵּם בְּשִׁיר יָרוֹן,
》 will exult. 〈 in song 〈 the mute 〈 and then 〈 wrath, 〈 and also 〈 banish 〈 Pain

נְחֵנוּ בְּמַעְגְּלֵי צֶדֶק, שְׁעֵה בִּרְכַּת בְּנֵי אַהֲרֹן.[2]
》 of Aaron. 〈 the 〈 the 〈 heed 〈 of 〈 in the paths 〈 Guide
children blessing righteousness, us

Leader – בִּרְשׁוּת מָרָנָן וְרַבָּנָן וְרַבּוֹתַי, נְבָרֵךְ אֱלֹהֵינוּ שֶׁהַשִּׂמְחָה
〈 for this 〈 our God, 〈 let us 》 of the distin- 〈 With the
celebration bless gentlemen, rabbis guished people permission

בִּמְעוֹנוֹ, (וְ)שֶׁאָכַלְנוּ מִשֶּׁלּוֹ.
》 of what 〈 (and) 〈 is in
is His. we have eaten His abode

Others – בָּרוּךְ אֱלֹהֵינוּ שֶׁהַשִּׂמְחָה בִּמְעוֹנוֹ, (וְ)שֶׁאָכַלְנוּ מִשֶּׁלּוֹ.
〈 of what 〈 (and) 〈 is in 〈 for this 〈 is our God, 〈 Blessed
is His we have eaten His abode celebration

וּבְטוּבוֹ חָיִינוּ.
》 we live. 〈 and through
His goodness

Leader – בָּרוּךְ אֱלֹהֵינוּ שֶׁהַשִּׂמְחָה בִּמְעוֹנוֹ, (וְ)שֶׁאָכַלְנוּ מִשֶּׁלּוֹ.
〈 of what 〈 (and) 〈 is in 〈 for this 〈 is our God, 〈 Blessed
is His we have eaten His abode celebration

וּבְטוּבוֹ חָיִינוּ.
》 we live. 〈 and through
His goodness

(בָּרוּךְ הוּא וּבָרוּךְ שְׁמוֹ.)
》 is His Name.) 〈 and Blessed 〈 is He 〈 (Blessed

CONTINUE WITH BLESSING AFTER MEALS (P. 6).

---

(1) *Psalms* 113:2. (2) Cf. 23:3.

27 / SHEVA BERACHOS

AFTER *BIRCAS HAMAZON* A SECOND CUP IS POURED AND THE FOLLOWING SEVEN BLESSINGS ARE RECITED. THE FIRST SIX MAY ALL BE RECITED BY ONE PERSON OR DISTRIBUTED AMONG SEVERAL PEOPLE. WHOEVER RECITES A BLESSING SHOULD HOLD THE SECOND CUP AS HE RECITES.

1. **בָּרוּךְ** אַתָּה יהוה אֱלֹהֵינוּ מֶלֶךְ הָעוֹלָם, שֶׁהַכֹּל בָּרָא
⟨ Who has created everything ⟨⟨ of the universe, ⟨ King ⟨ our God, ⟨ HASHEM, ⟨ are You, ⟨ Blessed

לִכְבוֹדוֹ.
⟨⟨ for His glory.

(אָמֵן – All.)
⟨⟨ (Amen.)

2. **בָּרוּךְ** אַתָּה יהוה אֱלֹהֵינוּ מֶלֶךְ הָעוֹלָם, יוֹצֵר הָאָדָם.
⟨⟨ the Man. ⟨ Who fashioned ⟨⟨ of the universe, ⟨ King ⟨ our God, ⟨ HASHEM, ⟨ are You, ⟨ Blessed

(אָמֵן – All.)
⟨⟨ (Amen.)

3. **בָּרוּךְ** אַתָּה יהוה אֱלֹהֵינוּ מֶלֶךְ הָעוֹלָם, אֲשֶׁר
⟨ Who ⟨ of the universe, ⟨ King ⟨ our God, ⟨ HASHEM, ⟨ are You, ⟨ Blessed

יָצַר אֶת הָאָדָם בְּצַלְמוֹ, בְּצֶלֶם דְּמוּת תַּבְנִיתוֹ, וְהִתְקִין
⟨ and prepared ⟨ of his likeness, ⟨ of the semblance ⟨ in the image ⟨⟨ in His image, ⟨ the Man ⟨ fashioned

לוֹ מִמֶּנּוּ בִּנְיַן עֲדֵי עַד. בָּרוּךְ אַתָּה יהוה, יוֹצֵר הָאָדָם.
⟨⟨ the Man. ⟨ Who fashioned ⟨ HASHEM, ⟨ are You, ⟨ Blessed ⟨ for eternity. ⟨ a ⟨⟨ – from ⟨⟨ for building himself – him

(אָמֵן – All.)
⟨⟨ (Amen.)

4. **שׂוֹשׂ** תָּשִׂישׂ וְתָגֵל הָעֲקָרָה, בְּקִבּוּץ בָּנֶיהָ לְתוֹכָהּ
⟨ amidst her ⟨ of her children ⟨ through the ingathering ⟨⟨ – the barren ⟨⟨ and exult ⟨ May she rejoice intensely one –

בְּשִׂמְחָה. בָּרוּךְ אַתָּה יהוה, מְשַׂמֵּחַ צִיּוֹן בְּבָנֶיהָ.
⟨⟨ through her children. ⟨ Zion ⟨ Who gladdens ⟨⟨ HASHEM, ⟨ are You, ⟨ Blessed ⟨⟨ in gladness.

(אָמֵן – All.)
⟨⟨ (Amen.)

5. **שַׂמֵּחַ** תְּשַׂמַּח רֵעִים הָאֲהוּבִים, כְּשַׂמֵּחֲךָ יְצִירְךָ בְּגַן
⟨ in the Garden ⟨ Your creations ⟨ as You gladdened ⟨⟨ who are beloved, ⟨ the companions ⟨ Gladden intensely

שבע ברכות / 28

עֵדֶן מִקֶּדֶם. בָּרוּךְ אַתָּה יהוה, מְשַׂמֵּחַ חָתָן וְכַלָּה.
《 and bride. 《 groom 《 Who gladdens 《 Hashem, 《 are You, 《 Blessed 《 from days of old. 《 of Eden

(אָמֵן – All)
《 (Amen.)

6. **בָּרוּךְ** אַתָּה יהוה אֱלֹהֵינוּ מֶלֶךְ הָעוֹלָם, אֲשֶׁר בָּרָא
《 created 《 Who 《 of the universe, 《 King 《 our God, 《 Hashem, 《 are You, 《 Blessed

שָׂשׂוֹן וְשִׂמְחָה, חָתָן וְכַלָּה, גִּילָה רִנָּה, דִּיצָה וְחֶדְוָה,
《 delight, 《 pleasure, 《 glad song, 《 rejoicing, 《 and bride, 《 groom 《 and gladness, 《 joy

אַהֲבָה וְאַחֲוָה, וְשָׁלוֹם וְרֵעוּת. מְהֵרָה יהוה אֱלֹהֵינוּ
《 our God, 《 Hashem, 《 Soon, 《 and companionship. 《 peace, 《 brotherhood, 《 love,

יִשָּׁמַע בְּעָרֵי יְהוּדָה וּבְחֻצוֹת יְרוּשָׁלַיִם, קוֹל שָׂשׂוֹן וְקוֹל
《 and the sound 《 of joy 《 the sound 《 of Jerusalem, 《 and in the streets 《 of Judah 《 in the cities 《 let there be heard

שִׂמְחָה, קוֹל חָתָן וְקוֹל כַּלָּה, קוֹל מִצְהֲלוֹת חֲתָנִים[1]
《 of grooms 《 of the jubilance 《 the sound 《 of the bride, 《 and the voice 《 of the groom 《 the voice 《 of gladness,

מֵחֻפָּתָם, וּנְעָרִים מִמִּשְׁתֵּה נְגִינָתָם. בָּרוּךְ אַתָּה יהוה,
《 Hashem, 《 are You, 《 Blessed 《 of song. 《 from their feasts 《 and of youths 《 from their canopies

מְשַׂמֵּחַ חָתָן עִם הַכַּלָּה.
《 the bride. 《 with 《 the groom 《 Who gladdens

(אָמֵן – All)
《 (Amen.)

THE LEADER OF BIRCAS HAMAZON RECITES THE SEVENTH BLESSING WHILE HOLDING THE FIRST CUP:

7. **בָּרוּךְ** אַתָּה יהוה אֱלֹהֵינוּ מֶלֶךְ הָעוֹלָם, בּוֹרֵא
《 Who creates 《 of the universe, 《 King 《 our God, 《 Hashem, 《 are You, 《 Blessed

פְּרִי הַגָּפֶן.
《 of the vine. 《 the fruit

(אָמֵן – All)
《 (Amen.)

THE LEADER DRINKS SOME OF THE WINE FROM HIS CUP; THEN WINE FROM THE TWO CUPS IS MIXED TOGETHER AND ONE CUP IS GIVEN TO THE GROOM AND THE OTHER TO THE BRIDE. IT IS LAUDABLE FOR THOSE PRESENT TO DRINK A BIT OF WINE FROM THE כּוֹס שֶׁל בְּרָכָה, *CUP OF BLESSING,* SINCE IT WAS USED IN THE PERFORMANCE OF A *MITZVAH.*

---

(1) Cf. *Jeremiah* 33:10-11.

29 / BRIS MILAH — ZIMUN

ZIMUN FOR THE CIRCUMCISION FEAST / זימון לסעודת הברית

THIS ZIMUN IS RECITED BY THE LEADER HOLDING A CUP OF WINE

Leader — רַבּוֹתַי מִיר וֶועלֶען בֶּענְטְשֶׁען [רַבּוֹתַי נְבָרֵךְ].
Gentlemen, › let us › bless. ›[Gentlemen, › let us bless.]»

Others — יְהִי שֵׁם יהוה מְבֹרָךְ מֵעַתָּה וְעַד עוֹלָם.¹
Let › the Name › of › Hashem › be › blessed › from this time › until › eternity.»

Leader — יְהִי שֵׁם יהוה מְבֹרָךְ מֵעַתָּה וְעַד עוֹלָם.¹
Let › the Name › of › Hashem › be › blessed › from this time › until › eternity.»

נוֹדֶה לְשִׁמְךָ* בְּתוֹךְ אֱמוּנַי,* בְּרוּכִים אַתֶּם לַיהוה.
We give thanks › to Your Name › among › my faithful;* › blessed › are you › to Hashem.»

Others — נוֹדֶה לְשִׁמְךָ בְּתוֹךְ אֱמוּנַי, בְּרוּכִים אַתֶּם לַיהוה.
We give thanks › to Your Name › among › my faithful; › blessed › are you › to Hashem.»

Leader — בִּרְשׁוּת אֵל אָיוֹם וְנוֹרָא, מִשְׂגָּב לְעִתּוֹת בַּצָּרָה,
With the permission › of the Almighty ‹—fearful › and › awesome, » the › Refuge › in times › of trouble,

אֵל נֶאְזָר בִּגְבוּרָה, אַדִּיר בַּמָּרוֹם יהוה.
the Almighty › girded › with › strength, › the Mighty › on high »—Hashem.»

Others — נוֹדֶה לְשִׁמְךָ בְּתוֹךְ אֱמוּנַי, בְּרוּכִים אַתֶּם לַיהוה.
We give thanks › to Your Name › among › my faithful; › blessed › are you › to Hashem.»

Leader — בִּרְשׁוּת הַתּוֹרָה הַקְּדוֹשָׁה, טְהוֹרָה הִיא וְגַם פְּרוּשָׁה,
With the permission › of the holy Torah, » pure › it is › and also › explicit,

צִוָּה לָנוּ מוֹרָשָׁה,* מֹשֶׁה עֶבֶד יהוה.*
commanded › to us › as a › heritage,* › [by] Moses, › servant › of Hashem.*»

---

(1) *Psalms* 113:2.

◆§ Bircas HaMazon for Bris Milah

נוֹדֶה לְשִׁמְךָ — *We give thanks to Your Name.* There are indications that this song was recited by Polish Jews following *all* festive meals. With the passage of time, the custom was discontinued except at circumcisions, as the Sages teach (*Shabbos* 130a), have always been celebrated with great joy].

אֱמוּנַי — *My faithful.* The one who leads the group in *Bircas HaMazon* refers to his companions as *faithful*, people whose faith is in God.

מוֹרָשָׁה — *Heritage.* The Torah is the *heritage* of Israel. As such we are not free to neglect it or cede it to any other nation.

עֶבֶד ה׳ — *Servant* (lit. *slave*) *of Hashem.* A slave is totally the property of his master. He has

Others — נוֹדֶה לְשִׁמְךָ בְּתוֹךְ אֱמוּנַי, בְּרוּכִים אַתֶּם לַיהוה.
We give thanks ⟩ to Your Name ⟩ among ⟩ my faithful; ⟩ blessed ⟩ are you ⟩ to Hashem.

Leader — בִּרְשׁוּת הַכֹּהֲנִים הַלְוִיִּם, אֶקְרָא לֵאלֹהֵי הָעִבְרִיִּים,
With the permission ⟩ of the Kohanim, ⟩ [from] the tribe of Levi, ⟩ I call ⟩ upon the God ⟩ of the Hebrews,

אֲהוֹדֶנּוּ בְּכָל אִיִּים,* אֲבָרְכָה אֶת יהוה.
I will thank Him ⟩ unto all ⟩ islands,* ⟩ I will give blessing ⟩ to Hashem.

Others — נוֹדֶה לְשִׁמְךָ בְּתוֹךְ אֱמוּנַי, בְּרוּכִים אַתֶּם לַיהוה.
We give thanks ⟩ to Your Name ⟩ among ⟩ my faithful; ⟩ blessed ⟩ are you ⟩ to Hashem.

Leader — בִּרְשׁוּת מָרָנָן וְרַבָּנָן וְרַבּוֹתַי, אֶפְתְּחָה בְּשִׁיר פִּי וּשְׂפָתַי,
With the permission ⟩ of the distinguished people, ⟩ rabbis ⟩ and ⟩ and gentlemen, ⟩ I open ⟩ in song ⟩ my mouth, ⟩ and my lips,

וְתֹאמַרְנָה עַצְמוֹתַי, בָּרוּךְ הַבָּא בְּשֵׁם יהוה.
and proclaim ⟩ shall my bones, ⟩ Blessed ⟩ is he who ⟩ comes ⟩ in the Name ⟩ of Hashem.

Others — נוֹדֶה לְשִׁמְךָ בְּתוֹךְ אֱמוּנַי, בְּרוּכִים אַתֶּם לַיהוה.
We give thanks ⟩ to Your Name ⟩ among ⟩ my faithful; ⟩ blessed ⟩ are you ⟩ to Hashem.

IF TEN MEN JOIN IN THE *ZIMUN*, AMONG WHOM AT LEAST SEVEN ATE BREAD, GOD'S NAME (IN PARENTHESES) IS ADDED.

Leader — בִּרְשׁוּת מָרָנָן וְרַבָּנָן וְרַבּוֹתַי,
With the permission ⟩ of the distinguished people, ⟩ rabbis ⟩ and gentlemen,

נְבָרֵךְ (אֱלֹהֵינוּ) שֶׁאָכַלְנוּ מִשֶּׁלּוֹ.
let us bless [Him,] ⟩ (our God) ⟩ for we have eaten ⟩ of what is His.

Others — בָּרוּךְ (אֱלֹהֵינוּ) שֶׁאָכַלְנוּ מִשֶּׁלּוֹ, וּבְטוּבוֹ חָיִינוּ.
Blessed is [He,] ⟩ (our God,) ⟩ that we have eaten ⟩ of what is His ⟩ and through His goodness ⟩ we live.

Leader — בָּרוּךְ (אֱלֹהֵינוּ) שֶׁאָכַלְנוּ מִשֶּׁלּוֹ, וּבְטוּבוֹ חָיִינוּ.
Blessed is [He,] ⟩ (our God,) ⟩ that we have eaten ⟩ of what is His ⟩ and through His goodness ⟩ we live.

(בָּרוּךְ הוּא וּבָרוּךְ שְׁמוֹ.)
(Blessed ⟩ is He ⟩ and Blessed ⟩ is His Name.)

CONTINUE WITH BIRCAS HAMAZON, *BLESSING AFTER MEALS* (P. 6), UNTIL בְּעֵינֵי אֱלֹהִים וְאָדָם, *IN THE EYES OF GOD AND MAN*, (P. 19).

---

neither personality nor initiative of his own. Moses is honored with this title because he was completely devoted to the will of God.

איים — *Islands*. The expression *islands* is used to indicate that the praise of God will be so universal that even the isolated inhabitants of far-flung islands will praise Him (see *Isaiah* 42:10 and *Malbim* there).

BRIS MILAH / HARACHAMAN

A DESIGNATED PERSON (OR PERSONS) RECITES THE FOLLOWING PRAYERS ALOUD.
SOMEONE OTHER THAN THE FATHER SHOULD RECITE THE FOLLOWING STANZA:

הָרַחֲמָן הוּא יְבָרֵךְ אֲבִי הַיֶּלֶד וְאִמּוֹ, וְיִזְכּוּ לְגַדְּלוֹ
The compassion- > May > bless > the > the child > and [the child's] mother; > and may > to raise
ate One! > He > father > they merit > him,

וּלְחַנְּכוֹ וּלְחַכְּמוֹ,* מִיּוֹם הַשְּׁמִינִי וָהָלְאָה יֵרָצֶה דָמוֹ,
to educate > and to make > from the eighth day > onward > may his blood
him, > him wise;* > > > find favor,*

וִיהִי יהוה אֱלֹהָיו עִמּוֹ.   (אָמֵן.–All)
and may > HASHEM, > his God, > be with him.   (Amen.)

SOMEONE OTHER THAN THE SANDAK SHOULD RECITE THE FOLLOWING STANZA:

הָרַחֲמָן הוּא יְבָרֵךְ בַּעַל בְּרִית הַמִּילָה,* אֲשֶׁר שָׂשׂ
The compassion- > May > bless > the > master > of the > covenant > of > who > was
ate One! > He > > > > > > circumcision,* > > joyful

לַעֲשׂוֹת צֶדֶק בְּגִילָה, וִישַׁלֵּם פָּעֳלוֹ וּמַשְׂכֻּרְתּוֹ כְּפוּלָה,*
to do > righteous- > with > rejoicing. > May he be > for his > and his > be doubled,*
> ness > > > rewarded > deed, > recompense

וְיִתְּנֵהוּ לְמַעְלָה לְמַעְלָה.   (אָמֵן.–All)
and may He > higher > and higher.   (Amen.)
place him

הָרַחֲמָן הוּא יְבָרֵךְ רַךְ הַנִּמּוֹל לִשְׁמוֹנָה, וְיִהְיוּ יָדָיו וְלִבּוֹ*
The compassion- > May > bless > the > tender one > who was > on the > and > his > and
ate One! > He > > > > circumcised > eighth day > may > strength > his heart*

לָאֵל אֱמוּנָה, וְיִזְכֶּה לִרְאוֹת פְּנֵי הַשְּׁכִינָה,* שָׁלֹשׁ פְּעָמִים
be faithful to God, > and may > he merit > to perceive > the Divine Presence,* > three > times

---

הָרַחֲמָן / The compassionate One!

לְגַדְּלוֹ וּלְחַנְּכוֹ וּלְחַכְּמוֹ — *To raise him, to educate him, and to make him wise.* "To raise him" physically by providing for his needs; "to educate him" by teaching him proper behavior and his obligations to God and people; "to make him wise" by teaching him the Torah.

מִיּוֹם הַשְּׁמִינִי וָהָלְאָה יֵרָצֶה דָמוֹ — *From the eighth day onward may his blood find favor.* Animals are acceptable for Temple offerings from the eighth day after birth. Thus, the blessing is that the eight-day-old infant be beloved to God from this eighth day of his life as if he were a holy offering.

בַּעַל בְּרִית הַמִּילָה — *The master of the covenant of circumcision.* This phrase refers to the san- dak, the one who held the infant while the circumcision was performed (*Maharil*).

וּמַשְׂכֻּרְתּוֹ כְּפוּלָה — *And his recompense be doubled.* He has participated in the physical act of circumcision, and he has done it joyfully. For each — the precept and the joy — he earns recompense (*Dover Shalom*).

יָדָיו וְלִבּוֹ — *His strength* (lit. *his hands) and his heart.* May he devote all his physical and intellectual abilities to God's service.

פְּנֵי הַשְּׁכִינָה — *The Divine Presence.* The juxtaposition of circumcision with God's Presence is based on an account in the *Zohar* which relates that God's Presence once departed from the Jews because an uncircumcised person mingled with them (*R' Reuven Margulies*).

בְּשָׁנָה.* 〉 a year.* 〉〉 (Amen.) — All〉 אָמֵן.)

SOMEONE OTHER THAN THE MOHEL SHOULD RECITE THE FOLLOWING STANZA:

הָרַחֲמָן הוּא יְבָרֵךְ בַּעַל בְּשַׂר הָעָרְלָה, וּפָרַע וּמָצַץ
〉〉 May 〈 The compassion- 〉 bless 〈 the one who 〈 the 〈 flesh 〈 the 〈 that was 〈〉 and 〈〉 and
He ate One! circumcised uncut, uncovered drew

דְּמֵי הַמִּילָה, אִישׁ הַיָּרֵא וְרַךְ הַלֵּבָב עֲבוֹדָתוֹ פְּסוּלָה,
〈 the 〈 of the 〈〉 A person 〈 who is 〈 and faint hearted, 〈 his service 〈〉 is unfit
bloods circumcision. fearful

(וְ)אִם שָׁלֹשׁ אֵלֶּה* לֹא יַעֲשֶׂה לָהּ. 〉〉 (Amen.) — All〉 אָמֵן.)
〈— (and) if 〈 these three [acts]* 〈 he does not perform 〈 upon it. 〉〉

הָרַחֲמָן הוּא יִשְׁלַח לָנוּ מְשִׁיחוֹ הוֹלֵךְ תָּמִים, בִּזְכוּת
〉〉 May 〈 The compassion- 〉 send 〈 us 〈 His 〈 who goes 〈〉 with 〈〉 in the
He ate One! anointed wholesomeness, merit

חֲתַן* לַמּוּלוֹת דָּמִים, לְבַשֵּׂר בְּשׂוֹרוֹת טוֹבוֹת וְנִחוּמִים,
〈 of the 〈 groom* 〈 [who] for the sake 〈 [is] 〉〉 〈 to proclaim 〈 good tidings 〈〉 and
circumcision bloodied, consolations,

לְעַם אֶחָד מְפֻזָּר וּמְפֹרָד בֵּין הָעַמִּים. 〉〉 (Amen.) — All〉 אָמֵן.)
〈 to the one nation 〈 dispersed 〈 and splintered 〈 among 〈〉 the nations.

הָרַחֲמָן הוּא יִשְׁלַח לָנוּ כֹּהֵן צֶדֶק אֲשֶׁר לֻקַּח לְעֵילוֹם,*
〉〉 May 〈 The compassion- 〉 send 〈 us 〈 the righteous 〈 who 〈 was 〈〉 into hiding,*
He ate One! Kohen* taken

עַד הוּכַן כִּסְאוֹ כַּשֶּׁמֶשׁ וְיַהֲלֹם, וַיָּלֶט פָּנָיו בְּאַדַּרְתּוֹ,*
〈 until 〈 established 〈 is His 〈 as sun 〈 [as bright] 〈 — diamond 〈〉 and 〈〉 he who 〈 his face 〈 with his
throne covered cloak*

וְיִגָּלוֹם, בְּרִיתִי הָיְתָה אִתּוֹ הַחַיִּים וְהַשָּׁלוֹם. 〉〉 (Amen.) — All〉 אָמֵן.)
〈〉 and enwrapped 〈 My 〈〉 was 〈 with him 〈 for life 〈 and peace. 〉〉
himself, covenant

ON WEEKDAYS CONTINUE הָרַחֲמָן הוּא יְזַכֵּנוּ, P. 20.
(ON THE SABBATH AND FESTIVALS, CONTINUE WITH THE APPROPRIATE PRAYER, P. 19.)

שָׁלֹשׁ פְּעָמִים בַּשָּׁנָה — *Three times a year*, on Pesach, Shavuos, and Succos, when Jews perceive the Presence of God in the Temple (Deut. 16:16). וְאִם שָׁלֹשׁ אֵלֶּה — *And if these three [acts]*. The three essential parts of the mitzvah: מִילָה, *circumcision*; פְּרִיעָה, *uncovering*; and מְצִיצָה, *drawing*.

חֲתַן — *Groom*. The word חָתָן, *groom*, in Hebrew refers to any honored person, whether it is a bridegroom or the infant being circumcised.

כֹּהֵן צֶדֶק — *The righteous Kohen* is the prophet Elijah who will herald the coming of the Messiah (Dover Shalom).

לְעֵילוֹם — *Into hiding*. Elijah was swept up to heaven while still alive (see II Kings 2:1), to remain concealed until the coming of the Messiah. Then Elijah will be revealed as if on a throne.

וַיָּלֶט פָּנָיו בְּאַדַּרְתּוֹ — *He who covered his face with his cloak*. When Elijah fled from the death threat of Ahab and Jezebel and hid in a cave, God came to him and he covered his face (I Kings 19:13).

THE BEDTIME SHEMA / קריאת שמע על המטה

רִבּוֹנוֹ שֶׁל עוֹלָם, הֲרֵינִי מוֹחֵל לְכָל מִי שֶׁהִכְעִיס
Master > of > the universe, > I hereby > forgive > anyone > who > angered

וְהִקְנִיט אוֹתִי, אוֹ שֶׁחָטָא כְּנֶגְדִּי – בֵּין בְּגוּפִי, בֵּין
antagonized > me > or > who sinned > against me > whether > against > whether
my body, or

בְּמָמוֹנִי, בֵּין בִּכְבוֹדִי, בֵּין בְּכָל אֲשֶׁר לִי; בֵּין בְּאֹנֶס,
against > whether > against > whether > against anything > that > whether > mine; > whether
my property, my honor is [he did so] accidentally,

בֵּין בְּרָצוֹן, בֵּין בְּשׁוֹגֵג, בֵּין בְּמֵזִיד; בֵּין בְּדִבּוּר, בֵּין
whether > willfully, > whether > carelessly, > whether > purposely; > or > whether > through > whether
speech,

בְּמַעֲשֶׂה, בֵּין בְּמַחֲשָׁבָה, בֵּין בְּהִרְהוּר; בֵּין בְּגִלְגּוּל זֶה,
through deed, > whether > in deliberation, > whether > with fleeting > or > whether > in this
thought; transmigration,

בֵּין בְּגִלְגּוּל אַחֵר – לְכָל בַּר יִשְׂרָאֵל, וְלֹא יֵעָנֵשׁ שׁוּם
or > in another > [I forgive] > every > Jew. > May not > be > any
transmigration; punished

אָדָם בִּסְבָתִי. יְהִי רָצוֹן מִלְּפָנֶיךָ, יהוה אֱלֹהַי וֵאלֹהֵי
person > because of > me. > May > it be > the will > before You, > Hashem, > my God > and the God

אֲבוֹתַי, שֶׁלֹּא אֶחֱטָא עוֹד, וּמַה שֶׁחָטָאתִי לְפָנֶיךָ מְחוֹק
of my > that I > sin > any- > What- > sins I > before > may You
forefathers, not more. ever have done You, erase

בְּרַחֲמֶיךָ הָרַבִּים, אֲבָל לֹא עַל יְדֵי יִסּוּרִים וָחֳלָיִם רָעִים.
in Your > that are > but > not > through > suffering > or > that
mercies abundant, illnesses, are bad.

יִהְיוּ לְרָצוֹן אִמְרֵי פִי וְהֶגְיוֹן לִבִּי לְפָנֶיךָ, יהוה צוּרִי וְגֹאֲלִי.¹
May > find > favor > the ex- > of my > and the > of my > before > Hashem, > my > and my
they pressions mouth thoughts heart— You, Rock Redeemer.

(1) Psalms 19:15.

❧ The Bedtime Shema

The recital of the *Shema* immediately before retiring is understood to be a protection against the dangers of the night (*Berachos* 5a).

The essence of the *Shema* is the *HaMapil* benediction and the first section of the *Shema*. The recital of the other psalms and verses are of ancient origin — many of the sources can be traced to the Talmud and the earliest halachic treatises such as *Kol Bo* (*Eliyah Rabbah*).

A full treatment of the Bedtime *Shema* appears in the ArtScroll edition of *Shema*.

❧ רבונו של עולם / Master of the Universe

Before retiring for the evening it is proper for

ברכת המפיל / HAMAPIL

בָּרוּךְ אַתָּה יהוה אֱלֹהֵינוּ מֶלֶךְ הָעוֹלָם,
Blessed are You, Hashem, our God, King of the universe,

הַמַּפִּיל חֶבְלֵי שֵׁנָה עַל עֵינָי, וּתְנוּמָה עַל עַפְעַפָּי.*
Who casts the bonds of sleep upon my eyes, and slumber upon my eyelids.*

וִיהִי רָצוֹן מִלְּפָנֶיךָ, יהוה אֱלֹהַי
May it be the will before You, Hashem, my God

וֵאלֹהֵי אֲבוֹתַי, שֶׁתַּשְׁכִּיבֵנִי לְשָׁלוֹם וְתַעֲמִידֵנִי
and the God of my forefathers, that You lay me down to sleep in peace and raise me up

לְשָׁלוֹם. וְאַל יְבַהֲלוּנִי רַעְיוֹנַי,* וַחֲלוֹמוֹת רָעִים
in peace. May I not be confounded by my ideas,* dreams that are bad,

וְהִרְהוּרִים רָעִים. וּתְהֵא מִטָּתִי שְׁלֵמָה לְפָנֶיךָ.
and fleeting thoughts that are bad; may my offspring be perfect before You.

וְהָאֵר עֵינַי פֶּן אִישַׁן הַמָּוֶת.*1 כִּי אַתָּה
and may You illuminate my eyes lest I sleep the [sleep of] death,*1 for it is You

---

(1) Cf. *Psalms* 13:4.

one to examine his deeds of that day; should one recall an improper deed he should pray for forgiveness and undertake to correct his ways. It is also proper for one to forgive those who have wronged him. In the merit of this, one will be granted long life (*Mishnah Berurah* 239 1:9). Accordingly, many recite this prayer before beginning the *Shema*.

‰ הַמַּפִּיל / HaMapil

There is a difference of opinion regarding the sequence of the prayers. Most *siddurim* — this volume included — place the HaMapil benediction first and then the *Shema*. This follows the order recorded by *Rambam* (*Hilchos Tefillah* 7:1). According to *Shulchan Aruch*, however, since HaMapil refers directly to the onset of slumber it should be recited, as close as possible to the moment of sleep, at the very end of the *Shema* service (*Orach Chaim* 239:1, apparently following the Talmud, *Berachos* 60b).

It is not proper to eat, drink, or talk after reciting the הַמַּפִּיל benediction; one should go to sleep immediately thereafter. One who cannot fall asleep should repeat the passages of the *Shema* and Psalms until sleep overtakes him (*Derech HaChaim; Aruch HaShulchan*).

הַמַּפִּיל חֶבְלֵי שֵׁנָה עַל עֵינַי וּתְנוּמָה עַל עַפְעַפָּי — *Who casts the bonds of sleep upon my eyes and slumber upon my eyelids*. This directly corresponds to the benediction recited in the morning: הַמַּעֲבִיר שֵׁנָה מֵעֵינָי וּתְנוּמָה מֵעַפְעַפָּי, *Who removes sleep from my eyes, and slumber from my eyelids*. There we thank God for returning us to active living; here we thank Him for the gift of sleep (*World of Prayer*).

The expression *bonds of sleep* figuratively depicts the whole body as being securely bound by sleep. Others render חֶבְלֵי שֵׁנָה as "portion" of sleep (see *Deut.* 32:9; *Chizkuni; Abudraham*).

וְאַל יְבַהֲלוּנִי רַעְיוֹנַי — *May I not be confounded by*

35 / THE BEDTIME SHEMA

הַמֵּאִיר לְאִישׁוֹן בַּת עָיִן.* בָּרוּךְ אַתָּה יהוה,
《 Hashem, 〈 are You, 〈 Blessed 《 of the eye.* 〈 the pupil 〈 Who illuminates

הַמֵּאִיר לָעוֹלָם כֻּלּוֹ בִּכְבוֹדוֹ.
《 with His glory. 〈 the entire world 〈 Who illuminates

THE SHEMA / שמע

אֵל מֶלֶךְ נֶאֱמָן.
《 Who is trustworthy. 〈 King 〈 God,

**RECITE THE FIRST VERSE ALOUD, WITH THE RIGHT HAND COVERING THE EYES,
AND CONCENTRATE INTENSELY UPON ACCEPTING GOD'S ABSOLUTE SOVEREIGNTY.**

שְׁמַע ׀ יִשְׂרָאֵל, יהוה ׀ אֱלֹהֵינוּ, יהוה ׀ אֶחָד:[1]
《 the One 〈 Hashem is 《 is our God, 〈 Hashem 〈 O Israel: 〈 Hear,
[and Only].

IN AN UNDERTONE:

בָּרוּךְ שֵׁם כְּבוֹד מַלְכוּתוֹ לְעוֹלָם וָעֶד.[2]
《 and ever. 〈 for ever 〈 kingdom 〈 of His 〈 is the 〈 Blessed
glorious Name

**WHILE RECITING THE FOLLOWING PARAGRAPH (DEUTERONOMY 6:5-9),
CONCENTRATE ON ACCEPTING THE COMMANDMENT TO LOVE GOD.**

וְאָהַבְתָּ אֵת ׀ יהוה ׀ אֱלֹהֶיךָ, בְּכָל־לְבָבְךָ,
〈 your heart, 〈 with all 〈 your God, 〈 Hashem, 〈 You shall love

וּבְכָל־נַפְשְׁךָ, וּבְכָל־מְאֹדֶךָ: וְהָיוּ הַדְּבָרִים הָאֵלֶּה,
〈 — these matters 《 They 《 your 〈 and with 〈 your soul, 〈 with all
should be resources. all

---

(1) *Deuteronomy* 6:4. (2) See *Pesachim* 56a.

my ideas. May the ideas and fantasies that we nurse in our wakeful hours not produce disturbing nightmares or immoral dreams. Such dreams menace the purity of our thoughts and feelings even during our waking hours (*World of Prayer*).

וְהָאֵר עֵינַי פֶּן אִישַׁן הַמָּוֶת — *And may You illuminate my eyes lest I sleep the [sleep of] death.* When asleep we are in a state related to death and utter darkness, but God guards our souls, as it were. We now beseech Him to return us to a state of vigorous sparkling light on the morrow lest our slumber becomes the sleep of death.

הַמֵּאִיר לְאִישׁוֹן בַּת עָיִן — *Who illuminates the pupil of the eye.* When one craves sleep, the pupils of his eyes are figuratively darkened; when one has slept and is fully rested, his eyes are "brightened" (*Abudraham*).

שמע / Shema

The halachah requires that only the first paragraph of *Shema* be recited at bedtime. However, one who recited *Maariv* before the stars were out should recite all three paragraphs again (*Aruch HaShulchan*, O.C. 239; see *Abudraham*; *Rashi*, *Berachos* 2a). *Magen Avraham* (O.C. 239:1) notes that it is desirable to recite all three paragraphs in any case.

אֲשֶׁר ׀ אָנֹכִי מְצַוְּךָ הַיּוֹם, עַל־לְבָבֶךָ: וְשִׁנַּנְתָּם
‹ Teach them ›› your heart. ‹ — upon ›› today ‹ command ‹ I ‹ that
thoroughly   you

לְבָנֶיךָ, וְדִבַּרְתָּ בָּם בְּשִׁבְתְּךָ בְּבֵיתֶךָ, וּבְלֶכְתְּךָ
‹ while you walk ‹ in your home, ‹ while you sit ‹ of them ‹ and speak ‹ to your children

בַדֶּרֶךְ, וּבְשָׁכְבְּךָ וּבְקוּמֶךָ: וּקְשַׁרְתָּם לְאוֹת ׀
‹ as a sign ‹ Bind them ›› and when you arise. ‹ when you lie down, ‹ on the way,

עַל־יָדֶךָ, וְהָיוּ לְטֹטָפֹת בֵּין ׀ עֵינֶיךָ: וּכְתַבְתָּם
‹ And write them ›› your eyes. ‹ between ‹ tefillin ‹ and they ‹ your arm ‹ upon
                                              shall be

עַל־מְזֻזוֹת בֵּיתֶךָ וּבִשְׁעָרֶיךָ:
›› and upon your gates. ‹ of your house ‹ the doorposts ‹ on

וִיהִי נֹעַם אֲדֹנָי אֱלֹהֵינוּ עָלֵינוּ; וּמַעֲשֵׂה יָדֵינוּ
‹ of our ‹ the work ›› be upon ‹ our God, ‹ of ‹ the ‹ May
hands,   Lord, pleasantness

כּוֹנְנָה עָלֵינוּ, וּמַעֲשֵׂה יָדֵינוּ כּוֹנְנֵהוּ.[1]
›› establish it. ‹ of our hands, ‹ the work ›› for us; ‹ establish

— Psalm 91 / תהלים צא —

יֹשֵׁב בְּסֵתֶר עֶלְיוֹן, בְּצֵל שַׁדַּי יִתְלוֹנָן.
‹ he shall ‹ of the ‹ in the [protec- ›› of the ‹ in the refuge ‹ Whoever
dwell. Almighty tive] shade Most High,   sits

אֹמַר לַיהוה: מַחְסִי וּמְצוּדָתִי, אֱלֹהַי אֶבְטַח
‹ I will trust ‹ my God, ›› and my fortress, ‹ [He is] my refuge ‹ of Hashem, ‹ I will say

בּוֹ. כִּי הוּא יַצִּילְךָ מִפַּח יָקוּשׁ, מִדֶּבֶר הַוּוֹת.
›› that is ‹ from ›› that ‹ from ‹ will deliver ‹ He ‹ For ›› in
devastating. pestilence   entraps, the snare you   Him.

בְּאֶבְרָתוֹ יָסֶךְ לָךְ, וְתַחַת כְּנָפָיו תֶּחְסֶה; צִנָּה
‹ [His] ›› you will ‹ His wings ‹ and ›› you, ‹ He will ‹ With His wing
shield find refuge;   beneath   cover

---
(1) *Psalms* 90:17.

THE BEDTIME SHEMA / 37

וְסֹחֵרָה אֲמִתּוֹ. לֹא תִירָא מִפַּחַד לָיְלָה, מֵחֵץ
and armor are His truth. You shall not fear the terror of night; [nor] the arrow

יָעוּף יוֹמָם. מִדֶּבֶר בָּאֹפֶל יַהֲלֹךְ, מִקֶּטֶב יָשׁוּד
that flies by day; [nor] the pestilence that in gloom walks; [nor] the destroyer who lays waste

צָהֳרָיִם. יִפֹּל מִצִּדְּךָ אֶלֶף, וּרְבָבָה מִימִינֶךָ, אֵלֶיךָ
at noon. Fall victim at your side may a thousand and a myriad at your right hand, but to you

לֹא יִגָּשׁ. רַק בְּעֵינֶיךָ תַבִּיט, וְשִׁלֻּמַת רְשָׁעִים
it shall not approach. Merely with your eyes will you peer, and the retribution of the wicked

תִּרְאֶה. כִּי אַתָּה יהוה מַחְסִי, עֶלְיוֹן שַׂמְתָּ
will you see. Because You, HASHEM, are my refuge, [in] the Most High have you made

מְעוֹנֶךָ. לֹא תְאֻנֶּה אֵלֶיךָ רָעָה, וְנֶגַע לֹא יִקְרַב
the abode of your trust. Not befall you will evil, and a plague will not come near

בְּאָהֳלֶךָ. כִּי מַלְאָכָיו יְצַוֶּה לָךְ, לִשְׁמָרְךָ בְּכָל
your tent. For He will command His angels for you, to protect you in all

דְּרָכֶיךָ. עַל כַּפַּיִם יִשָּׂאוּנְךָ, פֶּן תִּגֹּף בָּאֶבֶן רַגְלֶךָ.
your ways. On [their] palms they will carry you, lest you strike against a stone your foot.

עַל שַׁחַל וָפֶתֶן תִּדְרֹךְ, תִּרְמֹס כְּפִיר וְתַנִּין.
Upon the lion and the viper you will tread; you will trample the young lion and the serpent.

כִּי בִי חָשַׁק וַאֲפַלְּטֵהוּ, אֲשַׂגְּבֵהוּ כִּי יָדַע שְׁמִי.
Because for Me he has yearned and I will deliver him; I will elevate him for he knows My Name.

יִקְרָאֵנִי וְאֶעֱנֵהוּ, עִמּוֹ אָנֹכִי בְצָרָה; אֲחַלְּצֵהוּ
He will call upon Me and I will answer him, [together] with him am I in distress; I will release him

קריאת שמע על המטה / 38

וְאַכַבְּדֵהוּ. אֹרֶךְ יָמִים אַשְׂבִּיעֵהוּ, וְאַרְאֵהוּ
‹ and I will show him › ‹ I will satisfy him, › ‹ life › ‹ With long › ‹ and I will bring him honor.

בִּישׁוּעָתִי. אֹרֶךְ יָמִים אַשְׂבִּיעֵהוּ, וְאַרְאֵהוּ
‹ and I will show him › ‹ I will satisfy him, › ‹ life › ‹ With long › ‹ My salvation.

בִּישׁוּעָתִי.
‹ My salvation.

———— תהלים ג:ב-ט / Psalm 3:2-9 ————

יהוה, מָה רַבּוּ צָרָי, רַבִּים קָמִים עָלָי.
‹ against me! › ‹ rise up › ‹ Many › ‹ are my tormentors! › ‹ numerous › ‹ how › ‹ HASHEM,

רַבִּים אֹמְרִים לְנַפְשִׁי, אֵין יְשׁוּעָתָה לּוֹ בֵאלֹהִים
‹ from God, › ‹ for him › ‹ salvation › ‹ There is no › ‹ of my soul, › ‹ say › ‹ Many

סֶלָה. וְאַתָּה יהוה מָגֵן בַּעֲדִי, כְּבוֹדִי וּמֵרִים
‹ and the One Who raises › ‹ for my soul, › ‹ are a shield › ‹ for me, › ‹ HASHEM, › ‹ But You, › ‹ Selah!

רֹאשִׁי. קוֹלִי אֶל יהוה אֶקְרָא, וַיַּעֲנֵנִי* מֵהַר קָדְשׁוֹ
‹ from His holy mountain, › ‹ and He answers me* › ‹ I call out, › ‹ HASHEM › ‹ to › ‹ With my voice › ‹ my head.

סֶלָה. אֲנִי שָׁכַבְתִּי וָאִישָׁנָה, הֱקִיצוֹתִי,* כִּי יהוה
‹ HASHEM › ‹ for › ‹ yet I awoke,* › ‹ and I slept; › ‹ lay down › ‹ I › ‹ Selah.

יִסְמְכֵנִי. לֹא אִירָא מֵרִבְבוֹת עָם, אֲשֶׁר סָבִיב
‹ all around › ‹ that › ‹ of people › ‹ the myriads › ‹ I fear not › ‹ supports me.

Psalm 3 / ה׳ מָה רַבּוּ צָרָי ❊
This psalm was composed by David when he perceived through Divine inspiration that his salvation was forthcoming. Verse 6 — *I lay down and slept; yet I awoke, for* HASHEM *supports me* — makes this psalm especially appropriate for the night.

וַיַּעֲנֵנִי — *And He answers me* (lit. *He did answer*

me). The word literally is in past tense. David had such great confidence in God's response that whenever he prayed he was sure that his plea would be fulfilled. It was as if God had *already* answered his request (*Radak*).

הֱקִיצוֹתִי — *Yet I awoke.* From my worries I awoke triumphantly, filled with faith that God would support me (*Rashi*).

39 / THE BEDTIME SHEMA

שָׁתוּ עָלַי. קוּמָה יהוה, הוֹשִׁיעֵנִי אֱלֹהַי, כִּי הִכִּיתָ

Rise up, Hashem; save me, my God, for You struck against me. are deployed You

אֶת כָּל אֹיְבַי לֶחִי, שִׁנֵּי רְשָׁעִים שִׁבַּרְתָּ.

all of my enemies on the cheek. The teeth of the wicked You broke.

לַיהוה הַיְשׁוּעָה, עַל עַמְּךָ בִרְכָתֶךָ* סֶּלָה.

To Hashem is salvation, upon Your people is Your blessing,* Selah.

הַשְׁכִּיבֵנוּ יהוה אֱלֹהֵינוּ לְשָׁלוֹם, וְהַעֲמִידֵנוּ

Lay us down to sleep, Hashem, our God, in peace, and raise us up,

מַלְכֵּנוּ לְחַיִּים. וּפְרוֹשׂ עָלֵינוּ סֻכַּת שְׁלוֹמֶךָ,

our King, to life. Spread over us the shelter of Your peace.

וְתַקְּנֵנוּ בְּעֵצָה טוֹבָה מִלְּפָנֶיךָ, וְהוֹשִׁיעֵנוּ לְמַעַן

Set us aright with counsel that is good from before You, and save us for the sake

שְׁמֶךָ. וְהָגֵן בַּעֲדֵנוּ, וְהָסֵר מֵעָלֵינוּ אוֹיֵב, דֶּבֶר,

of Your Name. Shield us; remove from us foe, plague,

וְחֶרֶב, וְרָעָב, וְיָגוֹן, וְהָסֵר שָׂטָן מִלְּפָנֵינוּ

sword, famine, and sorrow; and remove spiritual impediment from before us

וּמֵאַחֲרֵינוּ, וּבְצֵל כְּנָפֶיךָ תַּסְתִּירֵנוּ,¹ כִּי אֵל

and from behind us, and in the shadow of Your wings shelter us. For God

שׁוֹמְרֵנוּ וּמַצִּילֵנוּ אָתָּה, כִּי אֵל מֶלֶךְ חַנּוּן

Who protects and rescues us are You; for God, King, Gracious

וְרַחוּם אָתָּה.² וּשְׁמֹר צֵאתֵנוּ וּבוֹאֵנוּ, לְחַיִּים

and Compassionate are You. Safeguard our going and our coming, for life

---

(1) Cf. *Psalms* 17:8. (2) Cf. *Nehemiah* 9:31.

עַל עַמְּךָ בִרְכָתֶךָ — *Upon Your people is* (their duty is) *Your blessing.* Your people are obliged to bless You and to offer thanks for Your salvation (*Rashi*). [God derives strength, so to speak, from the blessings and prayers of man. Man's appreciation of God's control of human events

וְלְשָׁלוֹם מֵעַתָּה וְעַד עוֹלָם.[1]
and for peace ⟩ from now ⟩ until ⟩ eternity. ⟫

בָּרוּךְ יהוה בַּיּוֹם, בָּרוּךְ יהוה בַּלַּיְלָה, בָּרוּךְ
Blessed ⟩ is Hashem ⟫ by day; ⟩ blessed ⟩ is Hashem ⟩ by night; ⟫ blessed ⟩

יהוה בְּשָׁכְבֵנוּ, בָּרוּךְ יהוה בְּקוּמֵנוּ. כִּי בְּיָדְךָ
is Hashem ⟩ when we retire; ⟫ blessed ⟩ is Hashem ⟩ when we arise. ⟩ For ⟫ in Your hand ⟩

נַפְשׁוֹת הַחַיִּים וְהַמֵּתִים. אֲשֶׁר בְּיָדוֹ נֶפֶשׁ כָּל
are the souls ⟩ of the living ⟩ and of the dead; ⟩ that ⟩ in His hand ⟩ is the soul ⟩ of all ⟩

חָי, וְרוּחַ כָּל בְּשַׂר אִישׁ.[2] בְּיָדְךָ אַפְקִיד רוּחִי,
living, ⟩ and the spirit ⟫ of all ⟩ mankind. ⟫ In Your hand ⟩ I shall entrust ⟩ my spirit, ⟫

פָּדִיתָה אוֹתִי, יהוה אֵל אֱמֶת.[3] אֱלֹהֵינוּ
You redeemed ⟩ me, ⟩ O Hashem, ⟩ God ⟩ of truth. ⟫ Our God, ⟩

שֶׁבַּשָּׁמַיִם, יַחֵד שִׁמְךָ וְקַיֵּם מַלְכוּתְךָ
Who is in heaven, ⟫ bring unity ⟩ to Your Name; ⟩ establish ⟩ Your kingdom ⟩

תָּמִיד, וּמְלוֹךְ עָלֵינוּ לְעוֹלָם וָעֶד.
forever ⟩ and reign ⟩ over us ⟩ forever ⟩ and ever. ⟫

יִרְאוּ עֵינֵינוּ וְיִשְׂמַח לִבֵּנוּ וְתָגֵל נַפְשֵׁנוּ
See ⟩ may our eyes, ⟩ ⟫ and be gladdened ⟩ may our heart, ⟫ and rejoice ⟩ may our soul ⟫

בִּישׁוּעָתֶךָ בֶּאֱמֶת, בֶּאֱמֹר לְצִיּוֹן מָלַךְ אֱלֹהָיִךְ.[4]
in Your salvation ⟩ in truth, ⟩ when it is told ⟫ to Zion, ⟩ Reigned ⟫ has Your God. ⟫

יהוה מֶלֶךְ,[5] יהוה מָלָךְ,[6] יהוה יִמְלֹךְ לְעֹלָם
Hashem ⟩ reigns, ⟫ Hashem ⟩ has reigned, ⟩ Hashem ⟩ shall reign ⟩ for ever ⟩

וָעֶד.[7] כִּי הַמַּלְכוּת שֶׁלְּךָ הִיא, וּלְעוֹלְמֵי עַד
and ever. ⟫ For ⟫ the kingdom ⟩ is Yours ⟩ ⟫ and for ever ⟩ and ever ⟩

---

(1) Cf. *Psalms* 121:8. (2) *Job* 12:10. (3) *Psalms* 31:6.
(4) Cf. *Isaiah* 52:7. (5) *Psalms* 10:16. (6) 93:1 et al. (7) *Exodus* 15:18.

---

influences His guidance of the universe.]

תִּמְלוֹךְ בִּכְבוֹד, כִּי אֵין לָנוּ מֶלֶךְ אֶלָּא אָתָּה.

will You reign ⟩ in glory, ⟩ for ⟩ we have no ⟩ King ⟩ except for ⟩ You.

הַמַּלְאָךְ* הַגּוֹאֵל אוֹתִי מִכָּל רָע יְבָרֵךְ

May the angel* ⟩ who redeems ⟩ me ⟩ from all ⟩ evil ⟩ bless

אֶת הַנְּעָרִים, וְיִקָּרֵא בָהֶם שְׁמִי,* וְשֵׁם אֲבֹתַי

the lads, ⟩ and ⟩ declared ⟩ upon ⟩ them ⟩ may my ⟩ name be,* ⟩ and the ⟩ of my
names forefathers

אַבְרָהָם וְיִצְחָק, וְיִדְגּוּ לָרֹב* בְּקֶרֶב הָאָרֶץ.¹

Abraham ⟩ and Isaac, ⟩ and like fish may ⟩ abundantly* ⟩ within ⟩ the land.
they proliferate

וַיֹּאמֶר, אִם שָׁמוֹעַ תִּשְׁמַע* לְקוֹל יהוה

He said: ⟩ If ⟩ you diligently heed* ⟩ the voice ⟩ of HASHEM,

אֱלֹהֶיךָ, וְהַיָּשָׁר בְּעֵינָיו תַּעֲשֶׂה, וְהַאֲזַנְתָּ

your God, ⟩ and that ⟩ in His eyes ⟩ you do, ⟩ and you listen
which is proper closely

לְמִצְוֺתָיו, וְשָׁמַרְתָּ כָּל חֻקָּיו, כָּל הַמַּחֲלָה

to His ⟩ and you ⟩ all ⟩ His decrees, ⟩ the ⟩ malady
commandments observe entire

אֲשֶׁר שַׂמְתִּי בְמִצְרַיִם* לֹא אָשִׂים עָלֶיךָ, כִּי

that ⟩ I inflicted ⟩ upon Egypt* ⟩ I will not inflict ⟩ upon you, ⟩ for

(1) Genesis 48:16.

◈§ הַמַּלְאָךְ — *May the angel.* The following passages are a collection of Scriptural verses discussing God's "mercy." This first verse, *May the angel who redeems*, etc. was Jacob's blessing to his grandsons Ephraim and Menashe (*Genesis* 48:16). The prayer is directed not to the angel, who has no power except as an agent of God, but to God Who dispatched the angel.

וְיִקָּרֵא בָהֶם שְׁמִי — *And declared upon them may my name be.* May they constantly strive to such heights that they will be worthy to have their names coupled with those of the Patriarchs (*R' Avraham ben HaRambam*).

וְיִדְגּוּ לָרֹב — *And like fish may they proliferate*

abundantly. R' Hirsch explains that just as fish enjoy contentment hidden from the gaze of human beings, so Jews who live in the sphere assigned them by God will have a degree of serenity and happiness far beyond the comprehension of those around them.

וַיֹּאמֶר אִם שָׁמוֹעַ תִּשְׁמַע — *He said, "If you diligently heed."* This passage forms the basis for the Talmudic statement [*Berachos* 5a] that Torah study, no less than the reading of the *Shema*, wards off danger (*World of Prayer*).

כָּל הַמַּחֲלָה אֲשֶׁר שַׂמְתִּי בְמִצְרַיִם — *The entire malady* (the plagues) *that I inflicted upon Egypt.* If the Jews remain faithful, they will be spared

אֲנִי יהוה רֹפְאֶךָ.[1]

≪ your Healer. ‹ HASHEM ‹ I am

וַיֹּאמֶר יהוה אֶל הַשָּׂטָן,* יִגְעַר יהוה בְּךָ
‹ O you, ‹ shall HASHEM ‹ Denounce ‹ the Satan,* ‹ to ‹ HASHEM said

הַשָּׂטָן, וְיִגְעַר יהוה בְּךָ הַבֹּחֵר בִּירוּשָׁלָיִם,
≪ Jerusalem. ‹ [HASHEM] Who chooses ‹ O you, ‹ shall HASHEM, ‹ and denounce ≪ Satan, again

הֲלוֹא זֶה אוּד מֻצָּל מֵאֵשׁ.[2]

≪ from a fire? ‹ rescued ‹ a firebrand ‹ this [man] ‹ Is not

הִנֵּה מִטָּתוֹ* שֶׁלִּשְׁלֹמֹה, שִׁשִּׁים גִּבֹּרִים סָבִיב
‹ encircle ‹ mighty ones ‹ Sixty ≪ of Shlomo! ‹ The couch* ‹ Indeed!

לָהּ, מִגִּבֹּרֵי יִשְׂרָאֵל. כֻּלָּם אֲחֻזֵי חֶרֶב, מְלֻמְּדֵי
‹ learned ≪ the sword, ‹ gripping ‹ All ≪ of Israel. ‹ of the mighty ones ‹ it,

מִלְחָמָה, אִישׁ חַרְבּוֹ עַל יְרֵכוֹ מִפַּחַד בַּלֵּילוֹת.[3]
≪ in the nights. ‹ from terror ‹ his thigh, ‹ on ‹ with his sword ‹ each ‹ in warfare,

RECITE THREE TIMES:

יְבָרֶכְךָ יהוה,* וְיִשְׁמְרֶךָ. יָאֵר יהוה פָּנָיו אֵלֶיךָ,
‹ for you ‹ May HASHEM countenance ‹ illuminate ≪ and safeguard you. ‹ May HASHEM Bless you*

וִיחֻנֶּךָּ. יִשָּׂא יהוה פָּנָיו אֵלֶיךָ, וְיָשֵׂם לְךָ שָׁלוֹם.[4]
≪ peace. ‹ for you ‹ and establish ‹ to you ‹ His countenance ‹ May HASHEM turn ≪ and be gracious to you.

(1) *Exodus* 15:26. (2) *Zechariah* 3:2. (3) *Song of Songs* 3:7-8. (4) *Numbers* 6:24-26.

---

physical affliction (Ramban).

וַיֹּאמֶר ה׳ אֶל הַשָּׂטָן — *HASHEM said to the Satan.* Satan had accused the high priest Joshua of being overly permissive with his sinful children and of hindering the rebuilding of the Temple. Thereupon God — Who chose Jerusalem — rebuked Satan, reminding him that Joshua had been Divinely vindicated inasmuch as he had been miraculously spared from the fires of Nebuchadnezzar. This metaphor also applies to the Jewish nation as a whole. It, too, is like a *firebrand rescued from a fire*, for it has suffered from the fires of exile and endured them.

הִנֵּה מִטָּתוֹ — *Indeed! The couch.* This passage refers allegorically to the Jewish people symbolized by the sixty myriads (the 600,000 battle-worthy males) who emerged from Egypt. See Commentary in the ArtScroll edition of *Shir HaShirim* for the full interpretation.

יְבָרֶכְךָ ה׳ — *May HASHEM bless you.* The

43 / THE BEDTIME SHEMA

RECITE THREE TIMES:

הִנֵּה לֹא יָנוּם וְלֹא יִישָׁן,* שׁוֹמֵר יִשְׂרָאֵל.¹

《 of Israel. 《— the Guardian 《 sleeps* 《 nor 《 slumbers 〈[He] neither 〈 It is so, that

RECITE THREE TIMES:

לִישׁוּעָתְךָ קִוִּיתִי יהוה.*² קִוִּיתִי יהוה
לִישׁוּעָתֶךָ. יהוה לִישׁוּעָתְךָ קִוִּיתִי.

《 HASHEM, 〈 I do yearn, 《 HASHEM.* 〈 I do yearn, 〈 For Your salvation
《 I do yearn. 〈 for Your salvation 〈 HASHEM, 《 for Your salvation.

RECITE THREE TIMES:

בְּשֵׁם* יהוה אֱלֹהֵי יִשְׂרָאֵל, מִימִינִי מִיכָאֵל,
וּמִשְּׂמֹאלִי גַּבְרִיאֵל, וּמִלְּפָנַי אוּרִיאֵל, וּמֵאֲחוֹרַי
רְפָאֵל, וְעַל רֹאשִׁי שְׁכִינַת אֵל.

《 may Michael be, 〈 at my right 〈 of Israel: 〈 God 〈 of HASHEM,* 〈 In the Name
〈 and behind me 《 Uriel, 〈 before me 《 Gabriel, 〈 at my left
《 of God. 〈 the Presence 〈 my head 〈 and above 《 Raphael;

———— Psalm 128 / תהלים קכח ————

שִׁיר הַמַּעֲלוֹת; אַשְׁרֵי כָּל יְרֵא יהוה,
《 HASHEM, 〈 who fears 〈 is each person 〈 Praiseworthy 《 of ascents. 〈 A song

הַהֹלֵךְ בִּדְרָכָיו. יְגִיעַ כַּפֶּיךָ כִּי תֹאכֵל, אַשְׁרֶיךָ
〈 you are praiseworthy, 《 you eat, 〈 when 《 of your hands, 〈 The labor 《 in His ways. 〈 who walks

(1) *Psalms* 121:4. (2) *Genesis* 49:18.

blessing contains sixty letters; this has significant Kabbalistic meaning as it parallels the sixty myriads of the previous passage.

עָס **הִנֵּה לֹא יָנוּם וְלֹא יִישָׁן** — *It is so, that [He] neither slumbers nor sleeps.* And therefore you will be able to sleep peacefully without fear of harm (R' Hirsch).

עָס **לִישׁוּעָתְךָ קִוִּיתִי** — *For Your salvation I do yearn, HASHEM*... The Kabbalists find in this three-word prayer mystical combinations of letters spelling the Divine Name that provides salvation from enemies. In order to arrive at the combination of letters yielding this Name, the three words of this prayer must be recited in three different orders (R' Bachya).

עָס **בְּשֵׁם ה'** — *In the Name of HASHEM.* God's angels surround you at His command: Michael, performing His unique miracles; Gabriel, the emissary of His almighty power; Uriel, who bears the light of God before you; Raphael, who

וְטוֹב לָךְ. אֶשְׁתְּךָ כְּגֶפֶן פֹּרִיָּה בְּיַרְכְּתֵי בֵיתֶךָ;
‹ of your home; › ‹ in the inner chambers › ‹ fruitful, › ‹ will be like a vine, › ‹ Your wife › ‹ with you. › ‹ and it is well

בָּנֶיךָ כִּשְׁתִלֵי זֵיתִים סָבִיב לְשֻׁלְחָנֶךָ. הִנֵּה כִי כֵן
‹ thus ‹ for › Indeed, › ‹ your table. › ‹ surrounding › ‹ of olive trees › ‹ will be like shoots › ‹ your children

יְבֹרַךְ גָּבֶר יְרֵא יְהוָה. יְבָרֶכְךָ יְהוָה מִצִּיּוֹן, וּרְאֵה
‹ and may you gaze › ‹ from Zion, › ‹ May Hashem bless you › ‹ Hashem. › ‹ who fears › ‹ the man › ‹ is blessed

בְּטוּב יְרוּשָׁלָיִם כֹּל יְמֵי חַיֶּיךָ. וּרְאֵה בָנִים
‹ children › ‹ And may you see › ‹ of your life.* › ‹ the days › ‹ all › ‹ of Jerusalem › ‹ upon the goodness

לְבָנֶיךָ, שָׁלוֹם עַל יִשְׂרָאֵל.
‹ Israel. › ‹ upon › ‹ peace › ‹ [born] to your children,

RECITE THREE TIMES:

רִגְזוּ וְאַל תֶּחֱטָאוּ,* אִמְרוּ בִלְבַבְכֶם עַל
‹ while on ‹ in your hearts › ‹ reflect › ‹ and do not sin;* › ‹ Tremble

מִשְׁכַּבְכֶם, וְדֹמּוּ סֶלָה.¹
‹ Selah. › ‹ and be utterly silent, › ‹ your beds,

---

(1) *Psalms* 4:5.

brings you healing from Him. Above your head is the Presence of God Himself (*R' Hirsch*).

⚡ רִגְזוּ וְאַל תֶּחֱטָאוּ — *Tremble and do not sin.* This verse exhorts Israel to tremble so greatly, at the thought of sin that the very idea of transgression becomes disturbing and traumatic (*Shaarei Teshuvah*).

The Talmud (*Berachos* 5a) interprets this verse homiletically: A person should constantly provoke his יֵצֶר טוֹב, *good inclination*, to battle against his יֵצֶר הָרָע, *evil inclination*, as it says, רִגְזוּ וְאַל תֶּחֱטָאוּ, literally, *provoke* or *agitate and do not sin*. If he succeeds in defeating the evil inclination, all is well. If not, he should engage in Torah study, as it says, אִמְרוּ בִלְבַבְכֶם, *"reflect in your hearts."* If he is victorious, all is well. If not, he should recite the portion of *Shema* [whereby one accepts the yoke of God's sovereignty] when he lies down to sleep, as it says, עַל מִשְׁכַּבְכֶם, *"while on your beds."* If he conquers, all is well. If not, he should remind himself of the awesome day of death, as it says, וְדֹמּוּ סֶלָה, *"and be utterly silent, Selah."*

45 / THE BEDTIME SHEMA

אֲדוֹן עוֹלָם* אֲשֶׁר מָלַךְ בְּטֶרֶם כָּל־יְצִיר נִבְרָא.
‹‹ Master ‹ of the universe* ‹ Who ‹ reigned ‹ before ‹ any ‹ form ‹‹ was created

לְעֵת נַעֲשָׂה בְחֶפְצוֹ כֹּל, אֲזַי מֶלֶךְ שְׁמוֹ נִקְרָא.
‹‹ was proclaimed. ‹ His Name ‹‹ as "King" ‹ then ‹‹ all things, ‹ when His will created, ‹ At the time

וְאַחֲרֵי כִּכְלוֹת הַכֹּל, לְבַדּוֹ יִמְלוֹךְ נוֹרָא.
‹‹ — the Awesome One. ‹‹ will reign ‹ He alone ‹ of all, ‹ the end ‹ After

וְהוּא הָיָה וְהוּא הֹוֶה, וְהוּא יִהְיֶה בְּתִפְאָרָה.
‹‹ in splendor. ‹ Who shall remain ‹ and He ‹ Who is ‹ and He ‹‹ Who was ‹ It is He

וְהוּא אֶחָד וְאֵין שֵׁנִי לְהַמְשִׁיל לוֹ לְהַחְבִּירָה.
‹‹ or to be His equal. ‹ to Him ‹ to compare ‹ second ‹ and there is no ‹ is One ‹ He

בְּלִי רֵאשִׁית בְּלִי תַכְלִית, וְלוֹ הָעֹז וְהַמִּשְׂרָה.
‹‹ and the dominion. ‹ is the power ‹ His ‹‹ conclusion, ‹ without ‹ beginning, ‹‹ Without

וְהוּא אֵלִי וְחַי גּוֹאֲלִי, וְצוּר חֶבְלִי בְּעֵת צָרָה.
‹‹ of distress. ‹ in a time ‹ from my pain ‹ a Rock ‹‹ Redeemer, ‹ my living ‹‹ my God, ‹ He is

וְהוּא נִסִּי וּמָנוֹס לִי, מְנָת כּוֹסִי בְּיוֹם אֶקְרָא.
‹‹ I call. ‹ on the day ‹ of my cup ‹ the portion ‹‹ for me, ‹ a refuge ‹‹ my banner, ‹ He is

בְּיָדוֹ אַפְקִיד רוּחִי בְּעֵת אִישַׁן וְאָעִירָה.
‹‹ — and I shall awaken! ‹‹ I go to sleep ‹ when ‹ my spirit ‹ I shall entrust ‹‹ Into His hand

וְעִם רוּחִי גְּוִיָּתִי, יהוה לִי וְלֹא אִירָא.
‹‹ I shall not fear. ‹‹ is with me, ‹ HASHEM ‹‹ my body shall remain; ‹ my spirit ‹ With

---

§ **אֲדוֹן עוֹלָם** — *Master of the universe.* Alternatively, *Master eternal.* This inspiring song of praise is attributed to R' Shlomo ibn Gabirol, who flourished in the 11th century. He was one of the greatest early *paytanim* [liturgical poets]. The song emphasizes that God is timeless, infinite and omnipotent. Mankind can offer Him only one thing: to proclaim Him as King, by doing His will and praising Him. Despite God's greatness, however, He involves Himself with man's personal needs in time of pain and distress. The prayer concludes on the inspiring note that, lofty though He is, *HASHEM is with me, I shall not fear.*

⊰{ WAYFARER'S PRAYER / תפלת הדרך }⊱

ONE SETTING OUT ON A JOURNEY RECITES THE FOLLOWING PRAYER ONCE HE LEAVES THE CITY LIMITS.

יְהִי רָצוֹן מִלְּפָנֶיךָ, יהוה אֱלֹהֵינוּ וֵאלֹהֵי אֲבוֹתֵינוּ,
≪ May it be ≻ the will ≺ before You, ≪ Hashem, ≺ our God ≻ and the God ≺ of our forefathers,

שֶׁתּוֹלִיכֵנוּ לְשָׁלוֹם, וְתַצְעִידֵנוּ לְשָׁלוֹם, וְתַדְרִיכֵנוּ לְשָׁלוֹם.
≪ that You lead us ≻ toward peace, ≪ emplace our footsteps ≻ toward peace, ≪ guide us ≻ toward peace,

וְתַגִּיעֵנוּ לִמְחוֹז חֶפְצֵנוּ לְחַיִּים וּלְשִׂמְחָה וּלְשָׁלוֹם.
≪ and make us reach ≻ the destination ≺ we desire ≪ for life, ≺ for gladness, ≻ and for peace,

ONE PLANNING TO RETURN THE SAME DAY ADDS:

[וְתַחֲזִירֵנוּ לְבֵיתֵנוּ לְשָׁלוֹם,] וְתַצִּילֵנוּ מִכַּף כָּל אוֹיֵב
≺ foe, ≺ of every ≺ the hand ≺ from ≺ May You rescue us ≻ in peace. ≺ to our homes ≺ and return us

וְאוֹרֵב (וְלִסְטִים וְחַיּוֹת רָעוֹת) בַּדֶּרֶךְ, וּמִכָּל מִינֵי
≺ manner ≺ and from all ≺ along the way, ≺ (that are harmful ≻ and animals ≺ bandits,) ≺ ambush,

פֻּרְעָנִיּוֹת הַמִּתְרַגְּשׁוֹת לָבוֹא לָעוֹלָם. וְתִשְׁלַח בְּרָכָה
≺ blessing ≺ May You send ≪ to earth. ≺ to come ≺ that assemble ≺ of misfortunes

בְּ(כָל) מַעֲשֵׂה יָדֵינוּ, וְתִתְּנֵנוּ לְחֵן וּלְחֶסֶד וּלְרַחֲמִים
≺ and compassion ≺ kindness, ≺ grace, ≺ and grant us ≺ of our hands, ≺ the work ≺ in (all)

בְּעֵינֶיךָ וּבְעֵינֵי כָל רוֹאֵינוּ, וְתִשְׁמַע קוֹל תַּחֲנוּנֵינוּ, כִּי אֵל
≺ a because ≺ God ≺ of our supplication ≺ the sound ≺ May You hear ≪ who see us, ≺ of ≺ and in the eyes ≺ in Your eyes

שׁוֹמֵעַ תְּפִלָּה וְתַחֲנוּן אָתָּה. בָּרוּךְ אַתָּה יהוה, שׁוֹמֵעַ
≺ Who hears ≪ Hashem, ≺ are You, ≺ Blessed ≺ are You. ≺ and supplication ≺ prayer ≺ Who hears

תְּפִלָּה.
≪ prayer.

EACH OF THE FOLLOWING PARAGRAPHS IS RECITED THREE TIMES:

וְיַעֲקֹב הָלַךְ לְדַרְכּוֹ, וַיִּפְגְּעוּ בוֹ מַלְאֲכֵי אֱלֹהִים.
≪ of God. ≺ did angels ≺ and encountered him ≺ on his way ≺ went ≺ Jacob

THE WAYFARER'S PRAYER

וַיִּקְרָא, זֶה אֱלֹהִים מַחֲנֵה רָאָם, כַּאֲשֶׁר יַעֲקֹב וַיֹּאמֶר
So he called ⟨⟨ is this. ⟨ that is Godly ⟨ A camp ⟨ he saw them, ⟨ when ⟨ Jacob said

מַחֲנָיִם.[1] הַהוּא הַמָּקוֹם שֵׁם
⟨⟨ Machanayim. ⟨ of that place ⟨ the name

הַנְּעָרִים, אֶת יְבָרֵךְ רָע מִכָּל אֹתִי הַגֹּאֵל **הַמַּלְאָךְ**
⟨⟨ the lads, ⟨ bless ⟨ evil ⟨ from all ⟨ me ⟨ who redeems ⟨ May the angel

וְיִדְגּוּ וְיִצְחָק, אַבְרָהָם אֲבֹתַי וְשֵׁם שְׁמִי, בָהֶם וְיִקָּרֵא
⟨ and like fish may they proliferate ⟨⟨ and Isaac, ⟨ Abraham ⟨ of my forefathers ⟨ and the names ⟨ may my name be, ⟨ upon them ⟨ and declared

הָאָרֶץ.[2] בְּקֶרֶב לָרֹב
⟨⟨ the land. ⟨ within ⟨ abundantly

יהוה לִישׁוּעָתְךָ. יהוה קִוִּיתִי) יהוה. קִוִּיתִי **לִישׁוּעָתְךָ**
⟨ Hashem ⟨⟨ for Your salvation. ⟨ Hashem, ⟨ I do yearn, ⟨⟨ Hashem. ⟨ I do yearn, ⟨ For Your salvation

קִוִּיתִי.) לִישׁוּעָתְךָ
⟨⟨ I do yearn. ⟨ for Your salvation

וְלַהֲבִיאֲךָ בַּדָּרֶךְ, לִשְׁמָרְךָ לְפָנֶיךָ מַלְאָךְ שֹׁלֵחַ אָנֹכִי **הִנֵּה**
⟨ and to bring you ⟨ on the way, ⟨ to protect you ⟨ before you ⟨ an angel ⟨ am sending ⟨ I ⟨ Indeed

הֲכִנֹתִי.[4] אֲשֶׁר הַמָּקוֹם אֶל
⟨⟨ I have prepared. ⟨ that ⟨ the place ⟨ to

בַשָּׁלוֹם.[5] עַמּוֹ אֶת יְבָרֵךְ יהוה יִתֵּן, לְעַמּוֹ עֹז **יהוה**
⟨⟨ with peace. ⟨ His nation ⟨ will bless ⟨ Hashem ⟨⟨ will give, ⟨ to His nation ⟨ strength ⟨ Hashem,

---

(1) *Genesis* 32:2-3. (2) 48:16. (3) 49:18. (4) *Exodus* 23:20. (5) *Psalms* 29:11.

Someone who sets out on a journey must pray that he arrive safely (*Berachos* 29b). This applies even if there is no reason to expect danger, provided that the distance will be at least one *parsah* (approx. 3 miles). The prayer should be recited as soon as one has gone about 140 feet past the last house of his town. In the event the entire journey will be less than one *parsah*, the prayer may be recited, but the concluding blessing (בָּרוּךְ אַתָּה ה' שׁוֹמֵעַ תְּפִלָּה, *Blessed are You, Hashem, Who hears prayer*) should be omitted. The prayer is recited once each day, even though the journey will be interrupted by rest, work, sightseeing, etc. However, if one's journey has ended, and he subsequently decides to embark on another journey on the same day, the Wayfarer's Prayer should be recited a second time. On a journey that will last for many days, the prayer is recited once each day.

It is preferable to recite a blessing before reciting the prayer so that it will be both preceded as well as concluded by blessings. Customarily this is done by consuming some food or drink and saying the final blessing. It is suggested that one eat a food that requires the final מֵעֵין שָׁלֹשׁ, *Three-faceted*, blessing and not בּוֹרֵא נְפָשׁוֹת, *Borei Nefashos*.

Although it is preferable to interrupt one's travel and to stand while reciting the prayer, this need not be done if it is difficult.

This volume is part of
THE ARTSCROLL SERIES®
an ongoing project of
translations, commentaries and expositions
on Scripture, Mishnah, Talmud, Halachah,
liturgy, history, the classic Rabbinic writings,
biographies and thought.

For a brochure of current publications
visit your local Hebrew bookseller
or contact the publisher:

Mesorah Publications, ltd

4401 Second Avenue
Brooklyn, New York 11232
(718) 921-9000
www.artscroll.com